MEMORY IN THE MIRROR

JANINE ELLIS-FYNN

© 2023 Janine Ellis-Fynn

All rights reserved. No part of this publication may be reproduced, stored in a retrieval system, or transmitted in any form by any means – electronic, mechanical, photocopying, recording or otherwise – without express written permission of the copyright holder.

Acknowledgments

Firstly, I'd like to thank Jesus Christ, my Lord and Saviour for giving me the idea to write *Memory in the Mirror.* Thank you to the Holy Spirit for breathing your life into my words.

I'd like to thank my husband, Kevin for his unwavering support in the writing of this book. He has always been my biggest fan and has encouraged me to stretch and grow. Kevin always challenges me to give my absolute best.

When I emerged from the cocoon and my wings were still wet, he sat next to me and showed himself to be a loyal and loving companion. Then when I could fly, he applauded me. I am so grateful for you, my love.

Thank you to Robert Harrison, my editor. You have done a wonderful job in making sure my manuscript is print ready. Your help is greatly appreciated.

Chapter One

First, let me tell you why I named my memoir *Memory in the Mirror*. As I sat down to write this book, I had to dig deep into my past and recall as many painful details as possible. I also had to look at myself in the mirror and really dissect what I saw. I've had to truly face myself head on. It has not been easy to delve into my past and write about it, but I can say that it has been cathartic. As I take you this journey of my life, I hope that you will be drawn to the One who loves you unconditionally. Honestly, I would not have made it without Jesus Christ, my Lord and Saviour.

On the cover of my book there is a colourful butterfly. You may ask why I put it there. Well, let me tell you. Over the years, God has spoken to me often about butterflies. When I have gone through excruciatingly hurtful times in my life, he has reminded me of the cocoon and shown me how pain can transform a lowly ground-crawling caterpillar into a beautiful butterfly.

The metamorphosis is a great mystery of nature and there is a lot we can learn from it. As you read my story, you will see how God has indeed done the same thing for me. He took me broken and ugly with sin, placed me in a cocoon for a long difficult season, and then showed his delight in me when I emerged as a beautiful butterfly. This was many years later once he had done his work in me.

God challenged me to write my story because there are so many caterpillars out there who need to hear it. Whatever stage in the process you are, God will meet you. Perhaps you are a caterpillar stuck in the vice of addiction, maybe you are in a cocoon of long-term sickness, maybe you have been betrayed and have become bitter and angry. Whatever your circumstances, God can come in and perform a miracle. If you let him, he will change you from a caterpillar into a beautiful butterfly. And the best news of all is that once your wings are dry, he will teach you how to fly.

My story began in Bulawayo, Rhodesia on the first of December 1968. Born wide eyed and expectant, I am the second child to my parents Clive and Tana Ellis. I have a brother, Vaughan, who is three years older than me. I lived with my family in Bulawayo for just a few short months until my parents moved to Salisbury. My dad was in the British South African Police and my mum was a nursing sister. Three years later, my little sister Leigh-Anne arrived.

I like to think that at some point my parents were happy. But unfortunately, I know very little about their early years. I know they loved each other but my dad didn't take well to the demands of fatherhood, and he always had a wandering eye which got him into trouble. My dad left the police and started a cosmetics company. When I was three years old, he had an affair with one of his models. According to the rumours, my mum saw him driving along in his convertible with a buxom blonde in the passenger seat. She confronted my dad and the whole ugly truth was revealed. My mum was devastated and promptly divorced him.

I have many fond memories of my childhood after the

divorce. My mum bought a lovely house on Clifton Road, Greendale which is in the eastern suburbs of Salisbury. It was on an acre of land, and we all loved living there. We had cats and dogs, rabbits, guinea pigs, a tortoise that I called Speedy Gonzales because he kept escaping from his enclosure; a handful of chickens and a very cheeky rooster who attacked me a few times. He eventually landed up in the pot for his sins and we enjoyed a very tasty lunch that day!

Vaughan was mad about collecting fish for his tank which he was very proud of. On Saturday mornings, once he had received his pocket money, he would cycle to the closest shopping center to buy more fish for his tank. He also loved fishing and on one occasion, whilst out with his friends, he caught a baby barbel (which is like a catfish). These fish live in the mud at the bottom of a riverbed and are not particularly friendly to other fish. When he came home with his trophy, I thought it would be a good idea to put the barbel in his fish tank with the other fish. This was not a very wise decision as the following morning there was a very smug looking barbel in the tank and not a single fish in sight. The barbel had eaten them all. I was not very popular after that!

Vaughan was a weekly boarder at Prince Edward High School, so my sister Leigh and I were without him during the week. He collected Dinky Cars and I loved taking them and making roads in the dirt in the garden. But I would always carefully clean them before putting them back on the shelf so that he wouldn't find out.

I was fascinated by Vaughan's motorbike and together with my friend Susan, from next door we secretly rode it whilst he was at school. But he cottoned on to this and ended up taking the keys to his bike to school with him. But I was determined so this didn't stop me. I used a pair of nail scissors to turn on the ignition and Susan 'borrowed' some petrol from her father's stash in his garage. We had a wonderful time riding around the garden on that 100cc motorbike.

As we had a sizeable garden, my mum decided we should install a pool. We watched with great excitement as the contractors dug an enormous hole and then filled it with cement. Once the water went in, we could not contain ourselves and went swimming before it was filled. A rock feature with a waterfall into the pool was added and we couldn't be prouder of our beautiful swimming pool. After that, we would swim from dawn to dusk. We just couldn't get enough of it.

Just a few meters away from the swimming pool there was a large Avocado Pear tree. Leigh and I loved to climb that tree. We would swing on the branches like little monkeys and then drop onto the soft bed of violets underneath. My mum was horrified that we kept flattening her plants and reprimanded us every time. But this didn't stop us. Leigh and I spent many hours playing in that big old tree.

My mum always organised the most wonderful birthday parties, complete with a novelty cake, musical chairs, pass-the-parcel, and lots of friends and family. I always looked forward to my birthday with great excitement. During those early years, my dad didn't feature much. I remember only seeing him on special occasions, such as birthdays or Christmas. But when I did see him, he always spoilt me rotten with gifts. But he was an enigma to me. I yearned to get to know him, as he was a stranger who occasionally visited. I only got this opportunity many years later.

I attended Courtney Selous School and absolutely loved it. Riding my bicycle to school and back every day made for some of the happiest days of my childhood. I was very active in athletics and often won certificates for the 100-metre sprint, or high jump. I was also good at hurdles and was always so proud when my mum attended the sporting events and cheered me on from the sidelines. My sports days were fraught with excitement and healthy competitiveness. I thrived in athletics and loved being part of 'Sable' house as we had a really good track record and always seemed to be on a winning streak.

When I was around twelve years old, my mum, siblings and I joined a Pentecostal Church. It was there that she met a man who would later become her husband. Edward, or 'Ted' as we called him was a butcher and had been married twice before. That should have been a red flag! After what felt like a whirlwind romance, Ted proposed to my mother and with delight she accepted. He was tall and handsome with penetrating blue eyes and a cockney accent. My mum seemed ecstatic, but I didn't like him one bit. I had huge reservations and he felt like an intruder into our happy little huddle.

Ted had a fetish for breeding canaries, and he built row upon row of little box cages for them. I was fascinated by the process of life and loved seeing the baby canaries hatch and then start to grow. I'm not sure why he enjoyed breeding canaries. I just assumed it was another odd trait which I found hard to understand. He was also passionate about Chow dogs (did you know they have black tongues?) Sherry was the first Chow we bought and a few months later we bought Bruno. Ted's intention was to breed them but unfortunately a Labrador got to Sherry first and she later gave birth to four rather odd looking but very cute puppies. It was around this time that I realised the caliber of man we were dealing with regarding Ted. The fourth puppy was born deformed, and he whisked it away and filled a plastic bag full of water, placed the puppy within it and drowned it. I was inconsolable!

For my mum's sake I really hoped that the marriage would last. Sadly, it did not. Ted had a drinking problem. I remember one evening sitting at the dining room table having dinner. Ted arrived home drunk as a skunk and promptly fell asleep with his face in his dinner. My long-suffering mum had to help him to bed, and she was very embarrassed by his odd behaviour. The drinking sprees became more regular, and, on another occasion, he passed out naked in the bathroom and I found him in that state. Not a very pleasant sight at all.

The worst part of it all was that Ted served as a Deacon in the Pentecostal Church we were attending. My siblings and I found it hard to stomach his hypocrisy and our dislike grew for him daily. He had three children from his previous marriage and on occasion they would come and visit their father. We all tried hard to get on with them but becoming a blended family was far harder than any of us expected.

Ted started having affairs just a couple of years into the marriage. I used to pray that everything would work out for us. Unfortunately, Ted's infidelities were the collective catalyst that caused my mum to have a mental breakdown. I think the reality that she was married for the second time to a man who betrayed her was just too much for her to bear. The heartbreak simply splintered her mind.

At around midnight one night, my mum woke my siblings and I up. 'Come, my feet are burning. I feel like I'm in hell. I think the rapture has happened. Get up and come with me,' she said. She was wide-eyed and clearly terrified. Vaughan, Leigh, and I all got out of bed and followed my mum outside. She went to the pool and stood on the first step. 'Come here.'

My siblings and I exchanged looks of utter bewilderment. What was going on? Reluctantly, we went to the pool and stood on the step with her. Then I noticed she had a needle in her hand. 'Give me your finger. I need to prick your finger.' I allowed her to do so and watched in dismay as a drop of blood appeared. What was she doing?

She did the same thing to Vaughan and Leigh, and then she climbed out of the pool. 'Come, we need to see if the neighbours have been raptured.' We followed her out of the pool. Barefoot and in our pajamas, we walked out of our house to the neighbour's house. My mum knocked on doors to find out if anyone was home. It was the most frightening occurrence I had ever experienced, and the memories would haunt me forever.

Eventually, an ambulance was called, and my mum was taken to hospital where she remained for three months. She was diagnosed with Temporal Lobe Epilepsy and given shock treatment or ECT. Back then the procedure was very barbaric and because of the shock treatment, she ended up with severe burns and chipped teeth. It was a very traumatic time for our family, and it took me years to forgive Ted for causing havoc and hurting my mum so deeply. What appalled me the most was that prior to Ted entering her life, my mother was happy, stable, and financially strong. She owned her home and had a good job. Ted on the other hand was penniless and simply owned his old noisy motorbike and the clothes on his back. So yes, I really do think that for him it was a marriage of convenience, and he was in it for what he could get.

Stepfather

I didn't invite you in, but you came anyway
Like a bulldozer on full throttle.
I wasn't sure how long you would stay,
I watched you with trepidation in my heart.
Knowing you would sooner or later depart,
I was only a child, but I saw through your mask.
The marriage of convenience could never last.
Shell-shocked mum and family ripped to shreds,
You gave to your lovers and left us the dregs.
When at last you packed up, there were no sad goodbyes,
Just relief and a lesson to always be wise.

Chapter Two

When my mum had her mental breakdown, it left me in a state of confusion and anxiety. I asked God how he could allow this to happen to her. It was a very disconcerting time as she was behaving totally out of character. She was hallucinating and believed she could see demons in the garden.

During the chaos of my mum's horrific breakdown, my sister and I decided to go into the little wooden shed in the garden and pray. I remember asking God not to take her away from us. But unfortunately, not even an hour later, an ambulance arrived, and my mum was taken to a psychiatric hospital. I remember feeling that God had failed me. Now, so many years later, I can look back on that time and realise that my ways are not God's ways. Even though it was traumatic for my siblings and I as children, God knew that my mum would receive the help she needed in a psychiatric facility.

Once my mum had been taken to hospital, rebellion and anger entered my heart. I simply could not understand why God had allowed such an awful tragedy to happen to her. I was confused and felt completely alone and wanted to scream. At the time we were living with my grandmother, and she was the one who had phoned for an ambulance. Now, as an adult, I wish I could go back and comfort that little girl who felt so abandoned. I would embrace her and calm her fears.

It was all made worse because nothing was ever explained to us. At no point did an adult sit us children down and tell us what was happening. We were just left floundering in the dark and trying to figure it all out for ourselves. When we did ask questions, we were told 'not to upset your mum.' The wrenching I felt when she disappeared to hospital was a physical feeling of acute loss and confusion. That she succumbed to the darkness of mental illness made it even more terrifying. At just twelve years old, I was ill-equipped to understand mental illness. I felt orphaned when she left, as my dad was not involved in my life at all. I remember resenting him for this. However, I can say that later down the line, he became more involved in the decision-making as to what would happen to us children every time my mum had a breakdown.

Although I was a Christian, I vented all my internal angst and confusion at God. I raged against him and asked him how he could allow something so horrific and tragic to happen to our family. The fact that my mum became extra over-the-top religious when she was in the throes of a mental breakdown scared me and completely put me off Christianity. Whilst she was having her second breakdown, I approached her to give her a hug. She slapped me across the face and said, 'Get away from me, Satan.' I have carried that moment all the years of my life as it burned deep into my soul. I can't even explain the level of sheer terror that I felt. No matter how much I dissected it and tried to make sense of it all, I always concluded that God did not care. If he did, he would never have allowed it to happen. It was only much later in my life that I could unravel it all and believe in a good God who cried with me at the injustice of it. Only once I was mature enough to comprehend God's infinite mercy, grace and love was I able to make peace with my past.

During my teens, I turned my back on God. Only later in my adult years did I come to see that even though I had walked away from him, he had not left my side. I was in so much turmoil and struggled to make sense of it all. Once my mum was well, we emigrated to Cape Town, South Africa. It was hard saying goodbye to all my friends in Zimbabwe, but I was also hopeful about starting a new life. My grandmother, Barbara who was also a divorcee, decided to move to Cape Town with us. I remember piling up her little blue Renault 4 and embarking on our big adventure. Unfortunately, a couple of months prior to the move, my mum had put all our furniture and worldly goods into a storage facility. Tragically, there was a fire and it all burnt to the ground. Arson was suspected but nothing was ever proven. All the family photos were burned and to this day I only have a couple of photos of myself as a baby and very few of me as a child.

After a two day, long and arduous drive through the scorching hot Karoo and onto the Garden Route we finally arrived in beautiful Cape Town. We were all very excited to see the sea and really believed that now our fortunes would change.

We moved into a lovely house just walking distance from Fishhoek beach. I was delighted that it had a pool too! I started school at Fishhoek High and for a few months, life in our new home was exciting and just what we needed. Little did I know that trouble was looming on the horizon. Just six months into our time in Fishhoek, my mum had another mental breakdown.

It started with her placing post-it notes all over the house with scripture verses written on them. I felt sick to my stomach as I recognised the symptoms from her previous breakdown. Later that day, my siblings and I were worried as when we came home from school, my mum wasn't back from work as expected. A few hours later, a friend of her's came to the house to tell us that my mum had been found trying to climb the mountain behind our house in her night dress! She was taken to Falkenberg Psychiatric Hospital. My siblings and I were devastated that she had suffered another breakdown. The breakdowns were becoming an annual occurrence. My Dad was contacted, and arrangements were made to fly Vaughan, Leigh, and I back to Zimbabwe to live with my dad whilst my mum recovered.

It was extremely difficult going back to the same school, Oriel Girls' High in Zimbabwe, when I had just left six months previously. This is when the lies started, as we were told by my dad to say simply that my mum was ill, but to not divulge that she had a mental illness. He was worried about the stigma attached to the words 'mental illness.' I remember feeling a deep sense of embarrassment and shame. I wish that I had been close to God then as it was a hard, lonely time, but I just couldn't seem to get past the sense of disappointment I had in him. It was too much for me to comprehend. The age-old question was burned into my mind. How could a good God allow such suffering? Where was he when it hurt? I was angry and confused and I blamed God.

Just before my siblings and I left Cape Town to return to Zimbabwe, we had visited my mum at Falkenberg Psychiatric Hospital. It was a traumatic experience for us, as she was catatonic and unresponsive. She did not even recognise her own children! I remember regretting seeing her in that state, as the memory would stay with me forever.

Living with my dad was challenging as he had a girlfriend Colleen who took an instant dislike to us. She was another buxom blonde with a hectic mouth on her and we often heard my dad and Colleen screaming at each other. I had nightmares that she may become my new stepmother as the relationship, although volatile seemed quite serious. My dad tried his best to look after us as best he could but sadly, I think he was just out of his depth. He relied on Colleen to mother us and that was a disaster. Colleen didn't have any children of her own and to be honest I always felt that she didn't have any sort of affinity with children. I remember her trying to reach out to Leigh and me. On one occasion, she bought ragdolls for us to decorate our beds, but we just took an instant dislike to the dolls, and they were hastily thrown in the cupboards.

My mum was at the psychiatric hospital for six months. Eventually, she got better and was released. My aunt Jeanette also lived in Cape Town, and she helped my mum to find a house near her in Plumstead. My siblings and I were told that we could return to South Africa to live with my mum again, as she seemed to be stable and had secured a good job.

We moved back to Cape Town and my sister and I were enrolled into Wynberg Girls' High School, which was situated close to where we lived. I found the transition difficult. The girls at my new school were cold and unfriendly and for my first six months there I was labelled 'the new girl' and was mocked because I could not speak Afrikaans. From a young age, I had found solace in the pages of a good book. In reading about the characters in a story, I was transported out of my miserable existence into a world where nothing bad ever happened.

So, during my lunch break times at Wynberg Girls' High School, I would sit under one of the large oak trees on my own and bury my head in a book. It took me six months to make any friends. I remember sitting there watching a frenetic little squirrel scurry up and down the oak tree gathering acorns. I wished I could be that squirrel. Free of hardship and pain.

In my second year at Wynberg Girls' High, I met Sharon, and we quickly became best friends. I would spend weekends at her house and her family embraced me like one of their own. Sharon and I would visit the roller-skating rink on the weekends. Parties were held there, so it became a favourite haunt for us. We had so much fun. It was there that I met my first boyfriend, Paul. I shared my first kiss with him but soon realised he wasn't right for me. The brief relationship lasted just three weeks before I broke it off with him.

Sharon and I were as thick as thieves, and we adored each other. We wrote letters and hung out with each other every opportunity we could find. Her parents were so warm and caring, and I would always look forward to spending the weekends at Sharon's house. Her mum and dad were Irish, so were full of warmth, fun and spirit.

It was around this time that I started smoking and drinking. At this stage, I was open to anything that would make me feel better. I had so much buried pain that alcohol numbed it and for a little while, I could forget about all my demons.

Chapter Three

When I was sixteen, my mum had yet another mental breakdown. Every year, strangely enough, around Easter time, she would get sick. For this reason, my dad decided it would be prudent to put Leigh and me in boarding school. So, we entered Wynberg Girls' High School hostel. I remember loving boarding school as it was the first time in many years that I felt even a remote semblance of security and stability. I made some wonderful friends whilst I was a boarder. As we were termly boarders, we were only allowed out on Sundays.

My aunt Jeanette was a lifeline at that time as she faithfully came to fetch us most Sundays and took us on outings. My mum lived in Wynberg not far from our school, but because she was in and out of hospital, we hardly saw her. Eventually, when I was seventeen and in my matric year, my mum recovered enough to secure a job. She moved to Stellenbosch and started working at the Health Hydro as a nurse. She flourished there and really enjoyed the job. For the first time in many years, she was relatively stable, and we began to plan a weekend out with her.

My mum phoned Miss Urie, the head mistress of the school

Memory in the Mirror

to ask if Leigh and I could come out for the weekend. But the answer was no! I still to this day do not know why the head mistress refused my mum. All I do know is that I was incensed with rage. How dare she prevent me from spending the weekend with my mum! I was angry and confused. Because I was in my final year, I had my own bedroom at boarding school. It was tiny, with a small window overlooking the grounds.

An idea began to form in my mind and eventually took root. I decided I would break out of boarding school and go drinking with my friends in an act of defiance towards Miss Urie. I shared my idea with a couple of my friends, and we arranged for some of our male friends from Wynberg Boys' High to wait for us in a car outside the school grounds. During dinner time, I pocketed a hostel teaspoon and once it was lights out and everyone had gone to sleep, my friend Sarah crept to my room. I proceeded to unscrew the burglar bars using the teaspoon.

I took off the burglar bars, and we climbed through the window and then raced across the grounds and climbed over the wall. Our friends were waiting for us, and we joined them in the car. We then drove to The Brass Bell, one of our favourite haunts in Kalk Bay. On a Friday night it was pumping with live music and a huge attendance. We had a few drinks and enjoyed ourselves and then later in the evening our friends returned us to the hostel. We crept back in without making a sound. I reattached the burglar bars and went to sleep.

We would have gotten away with our escapade if it wasn't for other boarders who found out about what we had done and started talking about it. No one had witnessed our escape, but it became big news in the hostel. I didn't know it, but I had an arch enemy, Jacqui, who saw the opportunity to bring me down a peg or two. She heard the news and went straight to her mum, who was on the committee of Wynberg Girls' High School. Her mum then reported us to Miss Urie.

Sarah and I were given a warning of expulsion and many, many hours of detention. I received an angry call from my dad as he had received a very stern letter from Miss Urie, mentioning the warning of expulsion. The only reason we weren't expelled was because in two short months we would be writing our final matric exams. Looking back, now I realise that because of my pain and anger, a spirit of rebellion had taken root in me, and this would be something I would struggle with for many years.

Miss Urie called us into her office separately and interrogated us. She wanted to know every little detail of our daring escape. How had we unscrewed the burglar bars? Did we use a hostel teaspoon? What time did we leave? What time did we get back? Who were we with? Where did we go? The questions were relentless. I guess Miss Urie just wanted to be sure that we were both telling the truth. Now, as a responsible adult, I can see just how reckless and foolish it was. I realise the difficult position I placed her in. I can see God's hand on my life as it truly was a miracle that I wasn't expelled from school.

After finishing my education at Wynberg, I got caught up in a crowd of school friends who smoked marijuana. I was still in so much pain and I found that by getting high, I could escape the torment. Being a bit wild during those days, my relationship with God took a back seat. I was angry with him and even though I knew deep down inside that it wasn't God's fault, I still felt let down and abandoned by him.

I had been brought up to believe that sex outside of marriage was wrong in God's eyes, but at this point in my life, I simply didn't care. So, after a long day spent on the beach getting high, we all went back to my friend, Heidi's house. We cooked the mussels we had picked from the rocks at the beach and smoked yet another joint. Much later in the evening, one of the guys, Ross made sexual advancements towards me and I lost my virginity to him. Looking back, I am very ashamed that I so carelessly threw my virginity away. But I realise that even then, God was watching and waiting to throw his arms around me and assure me he still loved me despite what I had done.

Virginity Lost

Red rose in a vase, the full bloom of youth,
Innocence bows to the sting of truth.
Lovers kiss and depart, let us not speak of this.
Who said we should wait for wedded bliss?

Petals crushed underfoot, bleeding and torn,
His honey smooth words disguising a thorn.
Tears of shame are lost on a sea of pain,
He had nothing to lose and everything to gain.

No backward glance or promise of tomorrow,
He will leave her to embrace her deep sorrow.
A lesson learned, she is crushed to the core,
There's no chance she can try to even the score.

Chapter Four

Whilst I was hanging out with my druggie friends, the unthinkable happened. Gavin, who I was particularly fond of, had an awful fight with his girlfriend and then committed suicide. I was beyond devastated and that's when I realised I needed to stop taking drugs and get my life back on track. My dad had said that he'd like me to come and live with him in Zimbabwe, so I jumped at the chance.

I really loved living with my dad and getting to know him better. We were really spoilt as he hired a chef to cook all our meals every morning. Papias would bring me boiled eggs, toast and tea in bed. It was heaven!

Although I had stopped taking drugs, I still was very involved in the nightclub scene and went clubbing almost every weekend. It was around this time that I met and fell in love with a guy who would change my life forever.

Gary was tall, dark, and handsome. I met him in Kariba whilst on holiday there with my brother. I was instantly smitten, and we started dating. One of our favourite places to visit on a Saturday night was Rosalind's, the nightclub where we would meet with all our friends. One Saturday night, Gary and I were invited to a party and the plan was to go to Rosalind's afterwards. At the last minute, Gary pulled out as he said he had to go to a modelling graduation of a friend. I was irked and jealous and wondered who this 'friend' was! Gary arranged for his friends to pick me up for the party and then told me he would meet me at Rosalind's after the graduation. I went to the party and then later arrived at the nightclub, but Gary was nowhere to be seen. I was devastated to be treated so appallingly by him, so I proceeded to drink too much to drown my sorrows. I was relying on Gary arriving to give me a lift home. When he still hadn't arrived in the early hours of the morning, I asked one of his friends to give me a lift home. Little did I know how this decision would impact my life.

Arthur agreed to give me a lift home and said he lived in walking distance of Rosalind's. So, I went with him. When we arrived at his house, I walked into the lounge and slumped into one of the chairs. I was so drunk at that stage. I remember thinking that it was odd that Arthur didn't turn on any lights when he walked into his house. Before I could fully comprehend what was happening, he had grabbed both my wrists with one hand and pulled up my skirt with the other and raped me. It was all over in a matter of minutes. I was numb with shock. I couldn't believe what had just happened to me! Arthur then called a taxi, and I cried all the way home. I was devastated.

Looking back, I wish I had reported the rape, but I was so ashamed for going to his house in the first place and I was worried that no one would believe me. It would be his word against mine. To make matters worse, Arthur phoned Gary the next morning and told him that I had consensual sex with him, so Gary phoned me and broke up with me!

I later found out that Gary's friends had made a bet to see

which of them could break us up. Apparently, Arthur won the bet. I was appalled!

The Rape of a Soul

Don't worry yourself, I'll take you home,
You were a friend; how could I have known?
Lust took my innocence, you showed me your hand,
I was gullible and young; how could I understand?

You raped my body and took what you could,
Intentions were clear, you were not misunderstood.
Your face I still see in the dark cloak of night,
But my Saviour has drawn me with his holy light.

I forgive the one who violated my trust.
Your body will die, and you will soon be dust.

Chapter Five

I buried the rape deep in the recesses of my mind and tried to get on with my life. The whole ugly experience left a bad taste in my mouth, and I wanted to escape from all the pain it brought. I didn't tell a soul and in part I blamed myself for going to Arthur's house. I kept telling myself that I should have known better. But I was a trusting eighteen-year-old and of course it never occurred to me that Arthur would use that opportunity to force himself on me.

I didn't realise it then, but hatred towards men burned within me like a simmering fire. It would be many years before I could find it in my heart to forgive Arthur. I have since learned that most rape victims remain silent as they are ashamed. So many heinous crimes go unreported, and the rapists get to continue walking the streets. I wish I had reported it to the police, but at the time I was just so ashamed and numb. Instead, I buried in deep in the recesses of my soul and tried to get on with my life. But many years later the pain would surface, and I would have to deal with it.

A friend of mine, Gayle had recently moved to the UK and

was loving living and working in London. So, she contacted me and invited me to come over and join her.

I had a friend, Claudia who was studying in Germany, and she had invited me to go skiing with her in Bavaria. So, before I flew to London, I arrived in Frankfurt and then took a train to Dusseldorf where my friend was waiting to meet me. I was just twenty years old, but ready to embrace the world and leave my troubles behind. I was beyond excited to try skiing for the first time. Claudia, her sister Dagmar, and I travelled from Dusseldorf to the ski resort, which was located a few hours away. It was an interesting experience as halfway to our destination; we had a flat tyre. It was snowing and freezing cold but us three young women managed to change the tyre and carry on with our journey. It was all part of an exciting adventure.

I enrolled in ski school whilst they took to the slopes. Once I had mastered the art of skiing, I joined the others, and I can honestly say that it was one of the most amazing, fun, and exhilarating experiences of my life.

After spending a month in Germany, I flew to London to begin my new life there. From the moment I arrived, I was enthralled. London was so different from any place I had ever known, and I felt like a kid in a candy store. Everything was new and exciting. I moved into a house share with five other people. We were a mixed bag of Zimbabweans, South Africans, and Australians. Fortunately, we all got on extremely well. I managed to find work easily and started my first job working for the BBC. I absolutely loved it and after my first week there, I bumped into the actress Joanna Lumley in the lift. As I was a huge fan of the television series *Absolutely Fabulous*, I was rendered quite speechless. I think all I did was smile admiringly at her. She must have thought I was a lunatic! But she was very gracious and just nodded and gave me a weak, dismissive smile. I suppose that being a celebrity, she was used to being admired by random strangers.

Although I had prayed about moving to the UK, I'm ashamed to admit that during those first few months in London, I barely gave God a second thought. I harboured deep resentment towards him over my mum's many mental breakdowns and, of course, the rape sealed it for me. I couldn't seem to get my head around the fact that God had allowed all that trauma to happen to me. At that stage, I didn't have a deep understanding of God's nature or of Satan's tactics and how he loves it when we resent God. It was only much later in my life that I came to understand that we live in a fallen world and bad things happen to good people.

I began to party hard with a couple of my house mates. We would go to a pub in Earl's Court and then on to a nightclub coming home in the early hours of the morning. All I knew was that the more I drank, the less the pain seemed to dominate my heart, soul, and mind. So, drink I did. I connected with JJ (Johannes Jacobus), one of the South Africans living in the house. I found him fascinating, not just in looks but personality too. He was very charismatic, with shoulder-length strawberry blonde hair that fell in ringlets around his face. He worked as a cameraman for the SABC and, like me, he had a penchant for reading, poetry, and philosophy. He also enjoyed the odd joint, so before I knew it, I fell into my old ways and would sit up late chatting to JJ about every topic under the sun and smoking marijuana.

When I look back now, I can see just how gracious God was during that time. As he gives us free will, he left me to my own devices, but the still, small voice deep inside my soul never completely disappeared. Often in the dead of the night, I could hear him cautioning me to be careful. He would also woo me with words of love, but I was still so angry that I simply ignored him.

I fell deeply in love with JJ. He was ten years older than me, so I admired his maturity and knowledge. Occasionally, we spoke about religion and his views were very New Age and the more I conversed with him and listened to his beliefs, the more interested I became. I was blind to God's incredible grace over my life as I was going astray. All I knew at the time was that Christianity hadn't worked for me, so I was open to trying something new. JJ and I would visit Camden Market and buy various books on philosophy and New Age. I would devour the books, as it was all so new and interesting to me. Little did I know that the enemy of my soul was slowly boiling me alive like a frog in a pot of hot water. I was too focused on how much I loved JJ and my life in London to care about God or what he was trying to tell me.

After a year of living in the house share, JJ and I decided to move in together. We found a quaint little two bedroomed house in Streatham and we were very excited to start our new life together. The next few months flew by, and I was the happiest I had been in long time. I had a great job in the city and was basically loving my life. I had shoved all the hurt so far down that I was sure I could keep a lid on it and only found out later just how wrong I was.

JJ went away to South Africa on a work project for six weeks and whilst he was gone, I met Jonathan. I was a member of the South Africa Club, which organised social events and functions for all South Africans living in the UK. But these parties also attracted a lot of Zimbabweans, Australians, and Kiwis. They were always great fun, and I was particularly looking forward to the next one, which was a *Rocky Horror Picture Show* themed party at the London Dungeons.

So, I went along with a few friends and had an absolute blast. Jonathan was from Pietermaritzburg, South Africa and was very handsome and charming, and flirted outrageously with me. I was appalled as he was there with his girlfriend.

'Jonathan, how can you flirt with me when you already have a girlfriend?'

'I can't help myself. I like you so much…you are the girl of my dreams.'

'If you want to talk to me, then I suggest you break up with your girlfriend first.'

I was having grave misgivings about JJ, as even though I loved him, I couldn't see myself marrying him. He was just too wild and unconventional and not the sort of man I felt comfortable bringing home to meet my family. Jonathan, on the other hand, was exactly the sort of man I could imagine marrying.

A few weeks went by and one weekend I went on another South African excursion on a coach to the coast. Jonathan was there.

He sauntered towards me with a swagger. 'Hey Janine, how are you doing?'

'I'm great, thanks Joe.'

'Well, I've broken up with my girlfriend now. So, will you come on a date with me?'

'Okay, that would be great.'

'Next Saturday. Meet me at Earl's Court tube station at around eight and I'll take you out to dinner.'

I had broken up with JJ and I truly believed I had met the man I would marry someday.

One date turned into two dates, and so it went on. My love affair with Joe blossomed. He would spoil me with gifts and tickets to the theatre. After a few months of being together, he begged me to move in with him. I was so enthralled with him that I agreed. By this stage, I was so smitten with him I would have walked to the ends of the earth for him. So, I moved into the flat he was sharing with another South African couple. We had many parties and good times in that flat and for the first few months, I was blissfully happy.

About six months into our relationship, I fell pregnant. I

remember doing the test with trepidation and trembling hands. I was on a contraceptive pill so when the test came out as positive, I was devastated. At the time, I had the flu and had been taking anti-biotics. Later, the doctor told me this can affect the efficacy of the pill. I waited for Jonathan to come back from work so I could share the news with him. When I told him, his face dropped.

'Janine, I'm not ready to have a child. How could this happen? I thought you were on the pill!'

'I am on the pill. The anti-biotics I am on must have affected it.'

'You need to make a plan.'

'I know. I'll sort it out.'

I was terrified of losing him, so I agreed to have an abortion. I was twenty-two years old at the time and Jonathan was twenty-eight. The next day I went into work and spoke to a colleague who I knew had recently had the procedure done. She gave me the telephone number of the Marie Stopes Clinic in London. At this point, I wasn't even considering God. I look back now and so wish I had consulted him. But I had become so hardened in my heart that I was no longer hearing that still small voice.

When I arrived at the clinic, I was ushered into the doctor's office and interviewed. I was asked a series of questions. Eventually, the doctor said he felt an abortion was the right route to go as I was not emotionally stable enough to have a child. He then told me it would just be a case of getting rid of a 'mass of cells.' I was then taken for an ultrasound scan, and I heard the baby's heartbeat! I remember thinking how on earth could the doctor say it was just a 'mass of cells' when I am sitting here listening to my baby's heartbeat?! What a cruel and deceptive contradiction. It felt as if the whole experience was happening to someone else. Almost as if I was outside of my body looking down. After the scan, I was taken into surgery and told that the procedure would just take an hour.

I woke up feeling a mixture of relief and regret. At that point, I had no idea how my life was about to change. Jonathan came to pick me up and he told me he had phoned his mum in South Africa, and she had said that we had made the right decision to get rid of the baby. I was devastated to hear that.

I tried to return to normal life, but I simply couldn't. I was consumed with regret and guilt. Every day I went to work and then came home and crawled into bed, crying for hours. Jonathan didn't know how to handle me, and we never spoke of the abortion again. I would dream about the baby that I felt I had murdered. Looking back, I wish I had turned to God at that point. But the truth was that the enemy had deceived me into thinking that I had committed a sin that was so huge that not even God could forgive me. I found it increasingly difficult to function. Every time I went into a grocery store, I would feel sick when I walked past the baby products. Every time I saw a baby, I wanted to cry. My arms ached to hold the baby I had lost. I was tormented day and night, and nothing gave me any sort of reprieve. I resented Jonathan for pushing me into the abortion and his lack of support afterwards. He did tell me that one day we would get married and have children, but this did little to ease my guilt and pain.

Eventually, Jonathan convinced me to see a psychologist. I reluctantly agreed. At the end of the session, the therapist told me I had a lost child inside of me. That was not news to me. I knew that after my traumatic childhood, anyone who knew me could come to that conclusion. It was a lot of money, and I didn't feel like it was worth it, so I didn't go back to the psychologist. I decided to try and manage my pain alone. I had felt alone my whole life, so why would it be any different now?

Time did little to ease the ache I felt inside. The weeks and months passed, but still I was consumed with grief over the abortion. I began to avoid social engagements and became very insular. At night in my dreams, I would hear my baby crying.

Little Boy Lost

Little boy running through fields of green and gold
Tears on a mother's face, motionless and cold.
Memories that will never be taunt from the grave,
While the Saviour whispers, 'I came to save.'

Regret like a coat hangs heavy 'tis true,
Frightened and alone, what could she do?
If only she'd known the loss she would feel,
Before the enemy came to rob and to steal.

She lives in hope for the day she will meet,
In paradise the child she couldn't keep.

I felt a lot of resentment towards the doctor at the Marie Stopes Clinic. I seethed with anger over the injustice of it all. The sheer evil of the practice itself. The lack of correct information.

Chapter Six

About six months after the abortion, I flew back to Cape Town, South Africa, to visit my mum. She had been ill again and suffered another mental breakdown but was out of hospital. I arrived in South Africa with a gaping wound in my heart, desperate to speak to her about it, but all the while knowing I couldn't as she was too fragile. I was with her for a couple of weeks, and I found it emotionally challenging. Once again, I had to be strong for her. My needs were not important. I simply had to bury them and remember that she was the fragile one. I remember deeply resenting her and feeling as if I were the parent. Deep inside I was crying out for a mother and the sheer desperation I felt was overwhelming at times. Not being able to rely on my mum or my dad, kept me in a vicious cycle of always feeling like an abandoned orphan.

I returned to London feeling cheated and desperately alone. Joe felt like a stranger to me, even though I was still living with him. I loved him and wanted to marry him, but I just couldn't understand how he could be so detached about the abortion. He took me on a holiday to Turkey. I think he hoped that it would take my mind off things. We had a wonderful time chartering a yacht for a week and exploring the coastline. I was enthralled with Turkey. I loved the culture and the beauty of it and for a while the voices in my head were silenced.

We returned to cold, bleak London and continued with our lives. Jonathan treated me to various West End musicals and shows, which I thoroughly enjoyed. He was very popular and had lots of friends, so there were always parties on the weekends and various sight-seeing excursions. Every time thoughts of the abortion surfaced, I would just tell myself that one day I would have a child with Jonathan and the pain would decrease. But deep down inside, I knew I was deceiving myself as I felt such a huge void in my soul that could only be filled with the child that I had murdered. In my mind, it was as simple as that.

After living in the UK for three and a half years, Jonathan and I felt the call to go home to South Africa. Joe wanted to return to his hometown, Pietermaritzburg. He told me that once we were settled there, we would get married. Whilst in London, we had done a fair amount of travelling and had really enjoyed our time there, but we felt the need to go back to South Africa.

We rented a little cottage in Pietermaritzburg, and we quickly settled into life there. But I found it challenging, as I didn't get on with Jonathan's mum. She was a hard, pretentious woman who was over-protective of her eldest son and suspicious of me. I tried to find a way for us to meet eye to eye, but we simply didn't like each other. This began to pose problems for Jonathan as he was very close to his mum and sought her opinion on absolutely everything. I realised that this would be a problem if I were to marry him. I certainly didn't want a mother-in-law who would interfere with our lives.

We had been living in Pietermaritzburg for about a year when Jonathan came home one evening and announced to me that our relationship was over. He looked at me with tears rolling down his cheeks and didn't even explain why exactly he was ending our relationship. In hindsight, I think it had a lot to do with his mother, but I don't know for sure. I was devastated. I moved out of the cottage and went to stay with my best friend, Felicity who lived close by. But I was a broken mess. I tried to keep it together for a few weeks but eventually realised that I would never be happy living in the same town as Jonathan. Pietermaritzburg is a small town and the chances of running in to him were quite high. So, I left my job and returned to Zimbabwe to live with my dad.

Whilst I was living in London, I had been diagnosed with severe depression and was prescribed Prozac. When I returned to Zimbabwe, I had been taking the medication for a few months, but my depression was no better. I was completely distraught over losing Jonathan and I couldn't seem to get over him. Then, three months after he had broken up with me, I heard via the grapevine that he had gotten engaged! I was horrified and it was then that I realised he must have been cheating on me whilst we were living in Pietermaritzburg.

I was completely crushed by the news. How could he do something so unbelievably cruel to me? I was still in a very fragile state of mind, and the news just tipped me over the edge. That night I returned home and took the entire box of Prozac. I was suicidal and I just wanted the pain to end. I remember driving my car and thinking how easy it would be to simply drive into the closest lamp post at full speed. But I was terrified of surviving a car accident and having horrific injuries, so I decided an overdose would be better. The thought of ending the pain was so alluring and I think Joe's betrayal burst open a wound that had been festering for a long time. All the pain came tumbling out and I couldn't cope with it. I felt so betrayed and abandoned and I couldn't believe Joe could do this to me. I had murdered my child to keep him and this I what I got in return. It was just too much to bear.

Jonathan

I was drawn in and enthralled with your easy way,
But what I saw in you I don't know to this day.

God in His mercy took me from you,
If I tried to work it out, I'd get in a stew.
Faithfulness so true I know he can tell,
the relationship would just cause sheer hell.

So, through bitter tears I thank God again,
for saving me from myself time and again.
I know my future is secure in his plan,
What anyone thinks I don't really care.
I'll follow him until he shows me the way,
And close by his side I will always stay.

I went to sleep that night hoping that I would never wake up. But the dosage I had taken was clearly not enough as the next day I woke up and all I had to show for my suicide attempt was a splitting headache. It was at this point that I knew I needed to turn back to God as he was the only person who could help me. So, I got dressed and drove down to the nearest church. I walked into the office of Highlands Presbyterian Church and told the pastor that I needed help as I had tried to kill myself.

He immediately referred me to Laurie, who was a trained Christian counsellor, and I immediately liked her the minute I met her. She was full of compassion and grace, and I was so grateful that I was finally getting the help I needed.

'Janine, I'm Laurie. It's very nice to meet you.'

'Hi Laurie, it's great to meet you too.'

'I'd like to see you once a week for the next couple of months. I have every confidence that God can heal you and restore you if you allow him to. How does that sound?'

'Perfect, thanks Laurie.'

Every week, for several months, I met with Laurie. She told me that God could and would forgive me for having an abortion. This was like water in a parched land for me. I could hardly believe that I could find redemption for the terrible sin I had committed. Going to the counselling sessions was the highlight of my week as I was hungry to learn more about God's grace and mercy. I recommitted my life to Christ, and I was thrilled that I could finally be free of the pain of the abortion.

'The first step is to forgive yourself, Janine. Do you think you can do that?'

'I want to…more than anything.'

'Then I want you to ask Jesus for his forgiveness. He is ready and waiting to extend grace to you. He loves you.'

I nodded. 'All this time I've been thinking that God would never forgive me. That I had committed the worst possible sin.'

'That's the enemy lying to you. He wants to convince you that you cannot receive redemption. But that is not the truth.'

'I want you to ask God to reveal the sex of your child to you. Then you can name him and find closure.'

'I've been praying, and God has already shown me that my child is a boy. I've decided to name him Matthew which means 'gift of God.'

'That's beautiful, Janine. Now can you ask your child for his forgiveness and then hand him over to Jesus.'

'Yes, I can do that.' I started to pray. 'Matthew, my beautiful boy, please forgive me for being so weak. I'm so sorry I didn't keep you. Please forgive me for ending your life.' I started to sob. 'I love you and I am handing you over to Jesus now. I know he will take good care of you.'

Every Sunday I attended church and grew close to God. For the first time in my life, I felt hopeful. I met loads of wonderful people and made friends who supported and encouraged me. I applied for a job as a copywriter at an advertising agency and I was thrilled when I got the job. It was a dream come true. After six months working as a copywriter, I was promoted to art director and before I knew it, I was working on television and radio campaigns, and I was having a ball. I was passionate about my work and even more passionate about my Lord.

Chapter Seven

I had been living in Zimbabwe for a couple of years when Keith, Jonathan's best friend, visited the country and asked to see me. I was reluctant but agreed to have coffee with him on a Saturday morning. I was curious as to why he wanted to see me but soon found out why he had come to Zimbabwe.

'How are you doing?' asked Keith. 'You look well.'

'I am well, thanks. Why are you here?'

'I'm here on business, and Joe asked me to look you up and find out how you are.'

'Well, as you can see, I'm great. How is Jonathan?'

'Not so good. He's very unhappy in his marriage. His wife is very controlling. He wants you back.'

I started to laugh. 'You've got to be kidding me. I am in a good place now and I'm very happy. I would never go back to him.'

'Okay, I'll tell him that.'

'Yes, please do.'

My life was full and happy. I was working in a job that I loved, and I was surrounded by many wonderful Christian friends who helped me grow in Christ and find my feet again. I went camping in Nyanga with my friends from church and it was there that I met Kevin. Little did I know at the time that he would later become my husband. Kevin and I immediately hit it off, and I spent hours discussing Christianity and other matters with him. I was drawn to him as he was very good looking, but I also found myself thinking that he was too young for me as he was four years younger than me.

I became very good friends with Richard and his sister Carla, who I met at church. We spent all our spare time together, and they taught me so much about God. We had a lot in common, as they had also had a traumatic past. We spent many hours discussing God and the incredible work he was doing in our lives. Sometimes we would go to the cottage that their dad owned in Nyanga. Those were some of the best times of my life. God really started to do a deep healing work in me, and I am so grateful for the wonderful friends that he sent me during that time.

I also found a great friend in Mike, who I also met at Highlands Presbyterian Church. We both loved playing squash so we would often book a court at the closest sports club and go and play on the weekend. But he was a far better player than me, so he usually won the match!

I continued to throw myself into my job. We were constantly pitching for new accounts, so sometimes I would work late into the evening. But I didn't mind as I enjoyed it. I loved the adrenalin rush of working towards a deadline and then getting the green light that the campaign had been approved. I was given more responsibility and oversaw both writing and directing various campaigns for television and radio. I had the most wonderful boss, and he really looked after me. He was always very appreciative of everything I did and gave me credit where it was due.

I had been with the advertising agency for three and a half

years when I started to struggle with my health. I noticed that I continually had flu like symptoms and swollen glands in my neck. I felt exhausted and out of sorts. My whole body ached and eventually I went to see a doctor to find out what the problem was. Blood tests were taken, and I was diagnosed with glandular fever. I wasn't too perturbed by the news, but my doctor told me I needed to be on bed rest for three weeks to shake the illness. I simply told her that this course of action was impossible as I had deadlines at work. I kept telling myself that I could handle the symptoms and just continue working. My doctor warned me that if I didn't slow down, the glandular fever could develop into chronic fatigue syndrome, and I could end up very sick. Still, I ignored her advice and carried on working.

I pushed myself hard and eventually the inevitable happened and I became very ill and ended up in hospital. My doctor confirmed that the glandular fever had now evolved into chronic fatigue syndrome and to get better, I would need to resign from my job. I was devastated! I passionately loved my job, and I couldn't imagine anything worse that having to leave it. I wrestled with this news for days, but after much deliberation, I reluctantly resigned.

My body seemed to just give up on me. The symptoms were now worse than ever. Splitting headaches, aching joints, swollen lymph glands and extreme fatigue. My doctor told me that if I wanted to recover fully, then I needed to be off work for at least a year! This was the very last news I wanted to hear. Fortunately, during this time, my dad was very supportive. He paid the rent for my flat and carried all my expenses. The frustrating part was that there was no cure for CFS. All I could do to get over it was rest and take lots of vitamins and minerals. During the next few months, I did extensive research on the illness so that I could be as informed as possible. I took every health concoction under the sun and followed a strict diet of no wheat, gluten, sugar, or preservatives. My friends rallied around and kept my spirits up, and slowly, over the next few months, I started to get better.

It was around this time that a friend of mine, Phil, told me he was getting a bunch of friends together to go skydiving. I loved the idea and told him to count me in. On a beautiful summer's day, we went to Mashonaland Sky Diving Club and did six hours of training before we jumped out of the small plane. When I finally plucked up the courage to jump, I fell into a cloud and for a few seconds, I was enthralled by the experience. It was incredible and when I landed, my hands were shaking from the sheer adrenaline of the experience.

Not long after this, a friend of mine who had been sexually abused as a child, and was also a Christian, phoned me. She told me she had heard of a course called The Wounded Heart that dealt with sexual abuse. Suzie asked me if I wanted to do the course with her, as she knew I had never fully dealt with the pain of the rape. I told her I would think about it. I decided to ask God and when I felt a nudging in my heart, I did the course. God showed me I still had so much pain that I had buried. Physically, I was feeling much stronger, but I still struggled with crippling fatigue. It made no difference how much sleep I had. Every morning I would wake up feeling exhausted, as if I had just run a marathon.

Chapter Eight

Regardless of how I was feeling, I decided to commit to doing the sexual abuse course. When I arrived at the counselling centre, it was a hive of activity. I sat down next to an attractive blonde woman who caught my eye and smiled.

'Hi,' I said. 'I'm Janine.'

'Hi, I'm Sonja. It's great to meet you.'

The facilitator of the group began to speak. 'Welcome everybody. My name is Cindy, and I will be leading the group. Let's go around the circle and find out everyone's name and then we'll get started.'

As the evening wore on, I was deeply touched by the stories that these beautiful women shared. They were unbelievably tragic. Sonja had been repeatedly abused by her own Father from a very young age. I shared my story and soon strong bonds began to grow between us.

When refreshments were served, Sonja said she was going outside for a cigarette. I said I would join her.

'How are you finding the course, Sonja?' I asked.

'It's very intense, isn't it? It's quite hard talking about the abuse.'

'Yes, and the fact that we have to dissect every detail is quite painful.'

'Are you a Christian, Sonja?'

'Yes, I am. I gave my life to Christ five years ago.'

'I made a commitment when I was twelve but backslid through my teens. It's a long story, so I won't go into it now. I've recently come back to God.'

I took a drag of my cigarette and then gently blew out the smoke. 'I can't believe I am smoking again. I gave it up, but I'm struggling with all the emotions I am feeling, so I just gave in.'

'We need whatever vices we can get right now,' said Sonja.

We finished our cigarettes and then returned to the meeting. Earlier, we had all shared our stories of sexual abuse, and now it was time for prayer.

'*Lord Jesus, thank you for being here with us this evening. Please bless every single brave woman who is sitting here. Bring healing and restoration. Fill them with your peace in Jesus' name.*'

Cindy began to speak. 'There's homework for you to do before our next meeting. You may find it heavy going as so many emotions will come up. But do it prayerfully and the Lord will help you. Next week, we will deal with forgiving the person who abused you.'

Sonja and I exchanged glances. I was completely at a loss as to how I would find the strength and grace to forgive the man who raped me. God would certainly have to help me, as I knew there was no way I could do it in my own strength.

Sonja invited me to dinner at her house the following evening. She had also asked a couple of ladies from the group who we had become friends with.

The following evening, when we were all together, we started discussing the Wounded Heart course.

I spoke first. 'I don't feel like I'm getting better since I started the course. In fact, I feel worse. I am so full of anger towards the man who raped me, and the pain is unrelenting. I felt better when the pain was buried. Now that it's surfaced, I can hardly bear it.'

Sonja nodded and then lit up a cigarette. 'I agree,' she said. 'I keep on having flashbacks and my depression is now worse than ever!'

Catherine was a small petite woman with short black hair.

'Maybe it's a case of it has to get worse before it can get better.'

'Well, it is certainly getting worse, that's for sure. I don't know if I can continue the course. It's just too painful,' I said, shaking my head. 'Reliving every detail is too much.'

We didn't go back to the course. I went back to my old ways of drinking, smoking, and visiting bars. The pain was back with a vengeance, and I did anything I could to numb it.

Around this time, Kevin phoned me. He was part of my church social crowd, so one of my friends gave him my number. I was pleased to hear from him.

'Hi, Janine, it's Kevin. How are you doing?'

'Hi, Kevin. It's great to hear from you. I'm well, thanks. How are you doing?'

'Good, I thought we could hang out some time. Can I come and visit you?'

'Yes, I would love that.'

I had heard via the Christian grapevine that Kevin had 'gone off the rails' as they put it. He was a Christian, but he too was in a lot of pain for various reasons so he, like me, had turned to alcohol and cigarettes to ease the pain. I was disgusted by the judgement he was receiving from so-called friends of his.

Kevin came to visit me, and we talked for hours about all sorts of topics. I felt comfortable with him, knowing he wasn't judging me, and I could relate to him. I understood why he was acting out and it was great to just completely be myself with him. At this point, we were just friends, and I had no romantic feelings towards him. But I was drawn to his beautiful soul, and I loved talking to him.

We enjoyed being together, and our friendship grew. I had one friend who warned me against Kevin. But I refused to listen. As far as I was concerned, he was the most down to earth, honest, and decent guy I had met in a long time. I understood him and my anger burned towards all those who judged him. We went to a mutual friend's wedding together and had a blast dancing and toasting the newlyweds.

Chapter Nine

Kevin quickly became my best friend and, after a few months, my feelings towards him started to change. I was very attracted to him and one evening, as we were saying goodbye to each other, we kissed. It was honestly the best kiss I had ever had. I fell into his arms and just wanted to stay there, finally feeling safe and seen. I had told him my darkest secrets and he had listened and understood. He was such a deep, sensitive person. He also had a dry wit and wicked sense of humour, so we spent a lot of our time laughing.

Kevin's childhood had been fraught with pain. His parents divorced when he was nine years old, and his dad remarried. The woman he married had three children from her first marriage, and Kevin's dad took them on and treated them like his own. Kevin and his sister Lindsay were raised by their mum with little or no involvement from their dad. Kevin had experienced a lot of rejection and he had anger issues towards his dad (something I could relate to).

Kevin told me he was planning on going to London to work and travel. Having done that myself, I was excited for him and told him he would love it. I was ambivalent towards his plans, as I knew I would miss him terribly, but I also wanted him to go and experience London the way I had.

I was very tearful when I said goodbye to Kevin. At this stage, I had developed feelings for him, and we had such a strong bond. He promised to stay in touch, and I said I would do the same.

Because I was still recovering from CFS, I hadn't worked in a year. But I was feeling much better and yearned to go back to work, yet London was calling to me once again. My friend Carla had recently gone over, and she said I could stay with her. So approximately a month after Kevin had left for the UK, I asked my dad if he could please pay for me to go back. My dad felt it was a wonderful idea and exactly what I needed.

Looking back, it warms my heart to remember just how amazing my dad had been during that time. I always had a tumultuous relationship with him as he was very critical and sometimes obnoxious. He wasn't one for flowery shows of affection and I don't remember him ever telling me he loved me, but when the rubber hit the road, he was always there for me. During my time living in Zimbabwe with him, we had grown closer and now that he has passed away, I am so eternally grateful for those memories.

I settled back into London life and enjoyed spending time with Carla who was one of my best friends. We had so much in common and we were very close. She was staying in her dad's flat and although she was happy for me to stay there for a few weeks, I didn't want to overstay my welcome. I was overjoyed to see Kevin who was also staying with a friend. He was sleeping on the couch, so was keen to find a place of his own. We met for coffee on a cold Saturday morning and looked through the newspaper for flats to rent. As we were both looking for accommodation, we agreed it would be a good idea for us to find a two-bedroomed flat to share. We eventually found one in Hanger Lane and about a week later, we moved in.

I found a job quickly, and Kevin and I settled into our new home. Kevin was working for an interiors company in Fulham, and he really enjoyed the work. His boss was a South African named Charles, and Kevin had become good friends with him. During this time, I was really struggling with my faith. I knew I had wandered so far from God and that I was 'living in sin' and I felt very guilty about it. To make matters worse, Kevin had started going out for drinks after work, sometimes for three nights in a row. I felt rejected and hurt. Our relationship started to unravel, and we fought frequently. Three months later, I returned to Zimbabwe to attend my sister's wedding.

It was wonderful to be back home again, and Leigh's wedding was beautiful. During the service, I was really convicted that I needed to stop sleeping with Kevin and return to God. I loved being able to catch up with family and friends and I really enjoyed the two weeks I spent back in Zimbabwe.

I returned to London and on my first evening back, Kevin pulled out all the stops. He had bought bunches of red roses and placed them all over our flat. Then he had done a candlelight dinner.

'I really missed you, Jay,' said Kevin.

'I missed you too, Kevin. But Leigh's wedding really convicted me. I want to do it God's way and right now we are living in sin. In the Bible, God is clear about it. No sex before marriage.'

'Yes, I know, Jay. But I'm not ready to get married yet.'

'Okay, I understand. But then we must break up.'

Chapter Ten

The following morning, Kevin moved out. I was heartbroken, but I had a peace in my heart that we were doing the right thing. I immediately started advertising for a flat mate, and I was pleased when an Australian girl contacted me. When I met her, I instantly liked her and after interviewing her, I offered her the room.

CFS is made worse by stress, so the next few months were difficult. I desperately missed Kevin and all the CFS symptoms had come back. After about six weeks, I phoned Kevin and asked him if he wanted to meet for a drink.

We met at the Fox & Goose, the local pub. I was so relieved to see Kevin and I struggled as I was so attracted to him. He had managed to rent a bedsit in Fulham, near his work. But I could see on his face that he was missing me, too.

'How have you been, Jay?' Kevin asked.

'I'm fine, busy at work. How are you doing?'

'Good, but I miss you.'

'I miss you too…what are we going to do?'

'I can start by inviting you to dinner at my place.'

'I'd love that…'

That weekend, I paid special attention to my appearance as I got ready for my date with Kevin. I was really looking forward to spending time with him. I arrived at his bedsit and when he opened the door, I was greeted with the rich aroma of roast chicken and garlic. Kevin opened a bottle of red wine and we sat and chatted for a while until the food was ready. Kevin is an excellent cook, so the food was delicious. When it was time to go, I stood up and reached for my coat.

'I had better get going.'

Kevin walked up to me and looked deep into my eyes.

'You know you don't have to go,' he said.

'I would love to stay here with you, but it just isn't right.'

'Let me give you a goodnight kiss, then.'

As soon as I felt Kevin's lips on mine, my passion was ignited. For weeks, I had suppressed my feelings and had tried desperately to get over him. But I was in love with him, and I just couldn't let him go. That night we made love with such tenderness and all thoughts of God were pushed aside.

But the following morning, I woke up feeling guilty. Once again, I had fallen, and I felt I had let God down. But one thing I knew for certain was that I couldn't stay away from Kevin. He was in my heart, and I didn't want to lose him.

We continued to go on dates. Occasionally, we had breakfast at a quaint little coffee shop in Fulham. I was constantly conflicted. I loved Kevin, but I also loved God and I knew that what I was doing was wrong. But I was addicted to Kevin and couldn't seem to tear myself away from him. Eventually, I just gave into my emotions and stopped trying to make sense of it all. My heart and mind were willing to obey God, but my flesh was weak.

Kevin was paying a huge amount of rent for his tiny little studio flat in Fulham and my flat mate had announced that she was going back to Australia. So, Kevin and I decided he would move back in with me. I was thrilled to have him home, and we celebrated with a wine and cheese evening. But I wasn't prepared for what he said next.

'Jay, I have to tell you something.'

'Okay, what is it?'

'After we broke up, I slept with another woman.'

'What? You must be kidding me. Who?'

'Abigail, a girl that I've been working with. But the relationship only lasted ten days. It was over when I invited you for dinner. I promise you.'

I was gutted. I couldn't believe that the Kevin I knew and loved could do such a thing! It wasn't surprising, though, as I had a suspicion that something was going on at work because of all the late nights and drinking sprees. I had sensed an attraction long before he acted on it. In fact, when I got on a plane to fly to Zimbabwe for Leigh's wedding, I had a strange feeling in the pit of my stomach that something awful was going to happen.

I wrestled with what to do. I loved Kevin and back then God spoke to me about the kind of man he was going to become. But I was struggling with the sting of betrayal. Although we had broken up when he had a relationship with another woman, I still felt desperately hurt and angry. I cried, I talked to God, I asked for guidance. Eventually I found peace and decided to forgive Kevin. He promised me that the relationship was over, and I just wanted to move past it. I asked God to give me the grace to put it behind me. Little did I know just how difficult that would be.

We carried on with our lives. I was happy in my job, and Kevin was still working for The Real Decorating Company. He was sent all over the world on various projects. One of them was Donna Karan's showroom in Japan. Kevin loved expanding his skills and, as he became known, he was heavily in demand. I think all the travelling helped to keep our relationship alive, as I missed him terribly when he was away. He was very excited when he was asked to fly to Saudi Arabia to work on one of the prince's palaces. It was a great opportunity for him, and he would be gone for six weeks.

Chapter Eleven

Whilst Kevin was away in Saudi Arabia, his boss Charles phoned me. I had met him once a few months ago and when we locked eyes, there was an instant attraction. But I dismissed it from my mind and thought nothing more about it.

'Hi, Janine, it's Charles. How are you doing?'

'Good. Thanks, Charles.'

'The reason I am phoning you is that I am having a party tonight and wondered if you'd like to come?'

'I'd love to. Thanks for inviting me.'

'Bruce and his brother are also coming. I've also invited Dawn, so you should know everyone.'

All the people attending the party were work colleagues of Kevin's that I had met before. I was feeling lonely without him, so I jumped at the opportunity to get out and socialise.

The party was in full swing when I arrived there. Charles welcomed me and offered me a glass of wine. I accepted and joined the others. During the evening, Charles kept on making eye contact with me. I was incredibly drawn to him as he was so cultured. We spoke about books, art, and philosophy. I found him incredibly attractive and as the wine flowed, my inhibitions started to wear thin. I drank far too much and eventually, one by one, the guests started to leave. It was obvious at this stage that Charles and I just wanted time alone. Never in my life had I experienced such a magnetic connection. I knew I was falling, and I didn't care at that point. Eventually the last guest left, and Charles and I gave into the mutual attraction between us. I had pushed Kevin to the back of my mind. When I woke up the following morning, I immediately regretted what I had done.

'Would you like to come away with me to the Lake District?' Charles asked.

'No, I have a feeling that Kevin is going to come back early from Saudi Arabia. I need to get home. How could I have done this? I love Kevin. Do you think it's possible to be in love with two people at the same time?'

'Yes, I do,' he answered.

I left Charles's apartment with my heart pounding in my chest. I was so conflicted. Part of me was still angry with Kevin for sleeping with another woman and I felt justified for what I had done. But the other part of me was angry with myself for giving in to my carnal desires. I felt both invigorated and alive, yet full of shame.

I was right about Kevin arriving that day. I was only expecting him back the following week, but for some reason he arrived later that same day. Bursting into the flat wearing an Arabian turban on his head, he was armed with all sorts of exotic presents for me. He gave me the most gorgeous perfume in an ornate bottle and a beautiful camel-bone jewelry box. He was full of stories about his time in Saudi Arabia, and I loved looking at all the photographs he had taken. Lots and lots of sand dunes and camels! It was great to have him home, but I felt sick to the stomach and knew I would have to tell him what I had done.

Later that evening, Kevin made sexual overtures towards me, and I just burst into tears. The guilt I was feeling was consuming me, so I told him what I had done. He was devastated and justifiably angry. I told him I had slept with another man, but I didn't tell him who, as I was too afraid of how he would react. I admit I was gutless and wrong to do that, but in the heat of the moment, I didn't know what else to do. As he had become good friends with Charles, I knew the news would crush him. So, I kept it hidden until I had the strength and courage to tell him the truth.

Now, I know the enemy operates when there are mistruths in our lives and at this stage, I had wandered so far from God that I really couldn't hear his voice. I think the fact that I had been unfaithful to Kevin evened the score in his mind. Although he was hurt and angry, he didn't break up with me. He told me he still loved me and wanted to continue with our relationship.

Kevin kept pressing me to tell me who I had slept with, and I told him I would tell him when I was ready. In the meantime, we planned a holiday away to Spain. We both felt like a getaway was exactly what we needed.

I was still struggling with thoughts of my time with Charles, as I had developed deep feelings for him. I wondered if I had done the right thing going back to Kevin. After all, he had betrayed me only a short few months ago.

It was great to get away from grey, dismal England and into the Spanish sunshine. We went to Costa Del Sol and loved exploring the quaint little town. But I was moody and irritable on the trip and couldn't seem to shake thoughts of Charles. I found myself wondering what would have happened had I gone to the Lake District with him. I realised I had not truly forgiven Kevin for sleeping with another woman. I was still hurt and angry, but I felt like a hypocrite as I had done the same thing to him.

I tried to focus on having a good time with Kevin and we did make some lasting, happy memories, but I was still so conflicted.

I realised I was, in fact, in love with two men at the same time. I hated feeling that way. I wanted to give myself wholeheartedly to Kevin, but I just couldn't seem to do it. Yet when I had been with Charles, I had thought about Kevin. I felt like a mess.

After two weeks in Spain, we returned to London and continued with our lives. I had told Kevin the truth about my illicit liaison, and he was so angry he confronted Charles. He left the Real Decorating Company and started working as a contractor for Armourcoat. We decided to put the past behind us and focus on the future. We spoke about having children and I told Kevin that I'd love to have a baby. He agreed and I guess we wished our first born into being as a couple of weeks later, I fell pregnant.

We discussed marriage, but I told Kevin that I didn't want him to marry me just because I was pregnant. I felt we should only get married if we truly believed we were right for each other and for no other reason. Despite pressure to get married from my family, we stuck by our guns. We also knew that many people were judging us, but we didn't care. We were going to do what was right for us and not placate family or friends.

Chapter Twelve

From early in the pregnancy, I sensed in my spirit that I was having a girl. I was delighted. Kevin and I discussed names and eventually decided on Rebecca Jade. Kevin was very supportive and attentive during the pregnancy and loved talking to my bump. When I was three months pregnant, I flew back to Zimbabwe to visit my mum. Her words to me when I arrived were, 'I have to find it in my heart to forgive you for falling pregnant!' I was gutted. She tried to convince me to stay in Zimbabwe and have the baby there, but I wanted to return to London instead. Once again, my mother had hurt me and let me down. My anger and resentment towards her burned within me. How could she be so insensitive and cruel? I realised that at the time all she was concerned about was her reputation amongst her church friends! She was ashamed of me and all I wanted to do was fly back to London and be with Kevin. At that stage in my life, he felt like the safest place to be.

After spending a month in Zimbabwe, I flew back to London. As my belly grew, I became excited to welcome my baby into the world. When I went into labour, Kevin drove me to the Queen Charlotte Hospital in Hammersmith and after a nine-hour labour, I gave birth to Rebecca Jade. She was the most beautiful baby girl I had ever seen. I was amazed by her mop of jet-black hair and her rosy, red lips. She was the image of Kevin.

From the moment I brought her home, Kevin was a hands-on dad. He gave Rebecca her very first bath and even though he was working long hours, he often got up in the middle of the night to attend to his daughter. My Mum had flown over for the birth, and she stayed with us for the first six weeks. It was an incredibly healing time for my mum and me because I felt that for once she was there for me in a practical sense.

The first six months were very difficult for me as I had severe post-natal depression. Kevin helped as much as he could, but he was working long hours and would arrive home exhausted every night. I eventually saw my GP and was given a prescription for anti-depressive medication, which helped me tremendously.

When Rebecca was about a month old, she developed colic. It was an incredibly stressful time for Kevin and me, as she would literally cry for hours. We would take turns trying to soothe her, but we realised we just had to ride it out. Then, after a couple of months, she simply grew out of it.

Apart from the colic, Rebecca was a delightful baby. After the colic disappeared, her little personality started to shine. She would smile a lot and we loved noting all her milestones. When Rebecca was six months old, Kevin's mum, Pauline came over to the UK to visit. It was lovely to have her, and she encouraged us to go out and have some quality time together whilst she babysat Rebecca.

On a Saturday morning, whilst we were having breakfast, Kevin told me his plans for the evening.

'Jay, I want to take you out to dinner tonight. We're going

somewhere nice, so dress up. I've booked a cab to take us to the restaurant.'

'Oh, how lovely,' I said.

We hadn't had a date night since Rebecca was born, so I was quite excited to be going out to dinner with Kevin. I wore a purple velvet and lace top with a long black skirt, and Kevin wore a suit. I was a little nervous about leaving Rebecca, but I knew she was in good hands with Pauline.

When it was time to go, we left our flat and walked outside to the road. I gasped when I saw a white limousine parked on the side.

'So, this is our ride,' I said with a big smile. 'How exciting.'

Kevin opened the door. 'There's a present for you inside.'

On the seat was a chilled magnum of champagne and two glasses!

'Ooh, how divine,'

'I thought you would like it.'

I felt like a celebrity. Kevin and I sipped from our glasses of champagne and enjoyed the drive from Ealing Broadway to the West End of London. The night views along the river Thames were magnificent and I just relished every moment of that journey. Eventually, we arrived outside the best Thai restaurant in London, The Blue Elephant. The restaurant was beautiful inside, with lots of orchids and exotic flowers on the tables. The staff were very friendly, and the food was sublime. It was such a treat to be out with Kevin, and I was in my element.

After we had finished our main course, Kevin looked me deep in the eyes with a smile tugging at the corners of his mouth.

'Jay, will you marry me?

My eyes misted over. 'Of course, I'll marry you, Kevin.'

A few weeks ago, we had been out shopping in Ealing Broadway and we had walked into a jewelry store. Kevin asked me which engagement ring I liked, and I pointed out a yellow gold eternity ring with seven diamonds. He opened the box and showed me the ring I had chosen. I was thrilled!

We ate dessert and finished our drinks. We then ordered coffee as we just didn't want the night to end. Everything about it was just so magical and I was so incredibly touched that Kevin had gone through so much effort to make our engagement truly special.

We enjoyed the journey back to our flat and when we walked inside, Pauline greeted us with excitement. Kevin had already told her he would be proposing to me that night.

'Congratulations! The ring is beautiful,' said Pauline.

'Thank you. It's exactly what I wanted.'

'How did it go with Rebecca?'

'She was an absolute angel. At eight I gave her a bottle, which she finished, and then I put her down. She's fast asleep. Tell me about your evening. Were you surprised, Jay?'

'I had a feeling Kevin was going to propose as he had gone through so much trouble to make it wonderful. But it was still a lovely surprise. The Blue Elephant is amazing. Such delicious food and excellent staff.'

'I'm so glad you both had an incredible evening. Did you take lots of photographs? I'd love to see them.'

'Yes, let me show you.'

After I had finished showing the photographs to Pauline, I went to check on Rebecca. She was fast asleep in her Moses basket. I remember looking at her and thinking how blessed I was. She looked like a little angel.

That night when I got into bed, I closed my eyes and prayed for the first time in a very long while.

Father God, thank you for Kevin. He's a good man and I'm so excited we are going to get married. Thank you, too for Rebecca. Help me to be a good mother to her. Bless her, in Jesus' name.

Chapter Thirteen

I decided it was time to go back to work. When Rebecca was six weeks old, I secured a job as a graphic designer for a printing company in our village, Pitshanger Lane. I had been out walking with Rebecca in her buggy when I saw the advertisement in the window, went inside, and was delighted to meet lovely young, South African couple who owned the business. I said I was very interested in the part time job, but I would have to get Rebecca into day care.

'Just bring your baby with you.' said Bridget. 'Your office will be downstairs in the basement, so you'll have all the privacy you need. The hours are ten to one.'

'Wow, that would be awesome. Thank you so much. Fortunately, Rebecca does sleep most of the time.'

I absolutely loved working for The Printing Press. I carried on with my work whilst Rebecca slept and when she woke up, I simply fed and changed her. I worked there for about four months, but eventually Bridget said business was booming and they needed someone to work for them full time. I looked at day care centres and I was horrified at the prices I found. Most of the money I earned would go toward paying for the day care. I visited one which was within walking distance from our flat. The centre was comprised of one large room packed full of babies and toddlers, most of whom didn't speak English. I was immediately put off and decided it was not right for Rebecca.

When Kevin returned home from work, I tearfully told him about my experience. This led to a conversation that would change the course of our lives.

'Love, it was just horrible. One room packed full of kids and no outdoor area for them to run and play. I want our children to grow up barefoot and playing outside like we did. And the worst part is that they charge a ridiculous amount of money too. By the time I've paid for daycare every month, I'm not going to have much money left.'

'I agree, Jay. Maybe we should start thinking about going home. You said you had a chat with Vaughan about moving to Joburg.'

'Well, we're going back to Zimbabwe to get married, so maybe we can move to South Africa afterwards.'

'Let me think about it,' said Kevin.

A few days later, Kevin told me he thought it would be a good idea to move to South Africa after the wedding. He too found the weather in the UK dismal, and he was longing for some sunshine.

We packed up all our belongings and arrived in Harare, Zimbabwe, the following week. I had just a couple of months to organise our wedding, so I got onto it straight away. Kevin and I had decided to keep our guest list as small as possible, so we only invited forty people. We wanted to get married in a beautiful garden, so we chose the Season's Restaurant which has the most magnificent grounds. The next couple of months flew by in a blur. A friend of mine, Adrienne, made my wedding dress, and she also made the bridesmaid and flower girl dresses. I was delighted with the finished products.

The day we got married dawned bright and sunny, and the gardens of the Season's Restaurant were looking glorious. Our wedding was magical, and it was so lovely to see all our friends and family again. At the end of our wedding ceremony, Rebecca was dedicated. She looked adorable in her white dress and sunflower ballet shoes. As sunflowers are my favourite flowers, I had them in my bouquet and in all the table arrangements.

After our wedding, one of the groomsmen, Bruce drove Kevin and me to the Meikles Hotel for the night. The following morning, we flew off to our honeymoon in Mauritius.

We had the most fantastic time on honeymoon. We went water-skiing, parasailing and scuba diving. The evenings were filled with scrumptious food and entertainment. We stayed at La Mauricia Hotel in Grand Bay, and we were thoroughly impressed by the excellent service and friendly staff. After the cold, grey weather of London, it was lovely to simply soak up the sun and enjoy ourselves. The two weeks we had in Mauritius flew by in a blur.

Kevin was delighted as he went deep sea fishing (a passion of his). But our tropical getaway was over too soon.

We returned to Zimbabwe and collected Rebecca from my mum's house. I had never been apart from Rebecca before, so although I loved my honeymoon, I had desperately missed her. Even in just two weeks, she had grown. We stayed in Zimbabwe for a couple of weeks before we moved to Johannesburg and rented a two bedroomed flat from my brother, Vaughan. Kevin and I enjoyed being back in Africa and welcomed the sunshine. I enrolled Rebecca in a daycare centre and Kevin, and I started searching for jobs. It proved to be more difficult than we expected as Kevin didn't have a South African identification document, so he couldn't work. But God was faithful, and he found some work paying cash until his documentation came through.

I started working at the Elmwood Media Group as a graphic designer and I took to it like a duck to water. It was a small advertising agency with some great accounts. The work was both challenging and rewarding, and Kevin and I soon settled into life in Joburg.

Rebecca started walking and before I knew it, I had a very active little toddler. She was delightful, and I cherished all her milestones. I wanted to hold on to and savour every moment with her. I found it stressful dropping her off at the daycare on my way to work as she always cried and clung to me. But the teacher at the daycare said it would only last a few minutes and then she would start playing with her friends. So that gave me a measure of comfort.

It was around this time that Kevin and I decided to buy a house. We eventually found a lovely home just down the road from where we had been living in Fourways. It was three bedroomed with a pool and a small garden and we both fell in love with it. We moved into our new house and for a while life was happy and uneventful. The months and years flew by and when Rebecca was three years old, she started asking us for a brother or sister. I was very keen to have another child, but Kevin needed a little more convincing. Eventually, he agreed we could go ahead and try for another baby. A few months later, I found out I was pregnant, and we were both delighted. Rebecca was thrilled, of course.

During this time, I was made redundant from my job at Elmwood Media Group. Kevin had gone into business with a man who we later found out was a con artist. We had invested all the money we had in the business venture and for three years, Kevin worked with Kobus to develop and market the business. When the writing was finally on the wall, we had lost a considerable amount of money and we also had to sell our house to survive that turbulent time.

Chapter Fourteen

On the twenty-sixth of December 2003, I gave birth to our second daughter, Gabriella Rose. She arrived a week early and was very ill when she was born. Whilst in the womb, she had developed a condition called myconium asphyxiation and she was rushed into neo natal as she was struggling to breathe. I remember feeling terrified that I was going to lose her. Kevin and I sent text messages out to all our family and friends, asking them to pray urgently for Gabriella. Kevin then went home to shower and for a few hours I was alone waiting to hear news about the wellbeing of our newborn baby. When Kevin returned to the hospital, we went up to neo natal to find out how Gabriella was doing.

The doctor showed us the x-rays of Gabriella's lungs. The black spots on the x-rays indicated she had pneumonia, and he said the next twenty-four hours were critical. He gave her a fifty percent chance of survival. It was heartbreaking seeing our tiny baby connected to a ventilator and heart monitor. She looked so vulnerable, and I had to blink back the tears as I watched her little chest rise and fall. I ached to hold her, and I was so sad that

I wouldn't be able to breastfeed her. She was put on formula and when we visited on her second day in neo natal, I was able to hold her and feed her. Right from such a tender age, Gabriella showed she was a little fighter. She gained weight and every day she improved. Eventually, after ten days in neo natal, the doctor gave her a clean bill of health, and we were able to take her home.

Gabriella

You burst into this world without a single cry,
just lay there gasping with a tiny sigh.
The nurses were alarmed and took you away,
you were very sick and couldn't stay.

With fear in my heart, I waited for news,
I was struck with a serious case of the blues.
You were admitted to ICU, and I could see you at last,
I cried for my tiny baby blinking through the glass,
linked to a ventilator I watched your little chest rise and fall,
As I waited for your dad walking down the hall.
We held hands and prayed for our daughter so dear,
And as God heard us, we felt our fear disappear.
Your progress was good and the nurses so kind,
But it was hard to go home and leave you behind.

Ten long days we waited as you fought hard to survive,
Each day inching closer to the place where you'd thrive.
Dawn broke and dispelled the dark cloak of night,
the end was here, it was finally in our sight.

You were given a clean bill of health at last,
the horror of pneumonia was now past.
Holding you close in my arms, I prayed,
thankful that God had with you stayed.

On the day that we could eventually take Gabriella home, my heart was just bursting with joy and gratitude. I knew in my spirit that God had spared her life and it had been a touch and go rollercoaster ride and I was utterly exhausted. It was so wonderful to cuddle her as much as I wanted to without the stark, austere surroundings of the hospital. She had gained weight, and the doctors had assured us she was completely healthy and ready to go home. She had a birthmark on her right thigh and later when she was older, I would tell her that it was where an angel had kissed her.

Although it was wonderful to have Gabriella at home with us, it was an incredibly tumultuous time. Kevin was still in business with a man who had conned us out of everything we owned. It was only during the next year that the full damage of this working relationship was revealed. I was furious as I had suspected very early in the relationship that he wasn't honest, and I had spoken of my fears to Kevin. The whole situation created a rift between us, and we couldn't seem to speak about it without erupting in a full-scale argument. Once the writing was on the wall that we had been conned, it was too late to salvage our finances. We also had a hefty hospital bill to pay and, as a result, we had no choice but to sell our house.

This was a bitter blow for us, and we reluctantly put our house on the market. At this point, I was an emotional wreck. I was trying to look after a baby plus figure out how to solve our financial crisis. I did a lot of praying during those difficult days, and God was very comforting.

It took six months for our house to sell and, as we were in a hurry, we had to sell it below its market value. That was devastating, but at least we could pay the hospital bill along with other debts we had accumulated.

To compound matters, we experienced the trauma of an attempted hi-jacking outside our house. Vaughan and his wife Wendy had invited Kevin and I out for dinner to celebrate my niece, Kimberley's, birthday. Vaughan had recently bought himself a brand-new Mitsubishi Pajero, and it was his pride and joy. On the evening in question, we left our children at our house in the capable hands of our trusted maid servant. We went out and enjoyed a lovely dinner, but as we pulled up to the gate of our house, two men emerged from the bushes. One of them held a gun to my brother's head and the other one held a gun to Kevin's head (he was sitting in the passenger seat). My mum, Wendy, and I were all seated in the back. We were told to exit the car, and the thieves took our mobile phones, watches, and some jewelry.

Whilst all this was going on, Rosie, our maid, popped her head around our front door and witnessed what was going on. She had the inclination to press the panic button and just in the nick of time, the alarm went out. The men ran away, and we were all grateful we had escaped with our lives. It could so easily have all gone another way, and I knew God was looking out for us.

After that horrendous experience, we were more certain that ever before that selling our house was the right move to make. The crime in our area had escalated, and we had also been burgled six months prior to the attempted high jacking. There were horrendous stories circling the airwaves of innocent homeowners who had been beaten, raped, and killed in Joburg.

Once our house was sold, we found a rental not far from where we were living. It was a delightful Victorian style townhouse in Lonehill, and I was really hoping that our little family could piece our lives back together once we moved in. I saw it as a new start and for the first few months, we were happy there.

I had decided that I didn't want to go back into full time work as I wanted to have time with Gabriella. So, I started my own graphic design business and called it Crimson Edge Design Studio. My ambition was to work from home around the demands of my two daughters. I was able to pick up a couple of great clients, and I soon had a steady flow of work to keep me busy.

Gabriella was a happy, contented baby who just smiled all day long. She was such a blessing, and I absolutely loved being able to be present during important milestones.

We had only been in our new home for about six months when we discovered that our neighbour, David was deeply disturbed. One day I came home from dropping Rebecca off at preschool and as I parked my car, David tapped on my window. I got the fright of my life. Thinking he wanted something, I rolled down my window and smiled at him. He proceeded to swear at me and curse me and then marched off to his house.

When Kevin came home from work, I told him about the incident, and he was incensed. He went to David's house and knocked on the door. Although we knew he was home as his car was in its parking bay, David did not answer his door. Instead, he leaned out of his window on the top floor and swore at Kevin.

During the next couple of months, we became friends with some of our other neighbours and it emerged that David was renown in the complex for causing trouble with the residents. We were told that he was a paranoid schizophrenic who smoked marijuana regularly. He was also homosexual, and rumour had it that his boyfriend had recently committed suicide. When I heard this, I immediately felt compassion for the man and decided that I would do my best to be friendly and polite to him.

The more we spoke to other residents at Lonehill Terrace, the more concerned we became. We heard horrendous stories of how David had stalked and terrorised residents and we were further dismayed to learn that he had a gun! I started to feel very unsafe in my own home and I feared for the safety of my children as I had caught him shouting at them on one occasion.

It escalated when David started following Kevin in his car and then accused us of being the Russian Mafia who were out to get him. David also lived a bizarre life where he seemed to sleep most of the day and then, during the evenings, he would pump up the volume of his music and knock on our lounge wall very loudly.

It was at this point that my mental health started to unravel, as between Gabriella waking me up at night and the incessant loud music, I wasn't getting much sleep. I was also trying to focus on work, and I had deadlines to meet, so sometimes I would work late into the night. Kevin and I weren't getting on very well as there was so much tension between us over losing our house. I must admit that I blamed him for going into business with a con man and although I tried hard to get past it, inside I was bitter and angry.

Having fallen away from God, I realised I should have sought him during that incredibly frightening and turbulent time. I felt very alone in my pain, and I kept having suicidal thoughts where I fully believed that my family would be better off without me. The emotional pain was intense, and I desperately wanted to be free of it, so I started down a dark road of seriously considering suicide. I felt soul tired and disillusioned and although I kept telling myself that I had two daughters who needed me, my mental health was so fragile that eventually I just snapped after I had an argument with Kevin.

I remember walking into my bedroom and opening my bedside drawer. I then took out all the medication I was on for depression and anxiety and took the whole lot. I lay down on my bed and willed sleep to come, telling myself that I was a burden to my family and that they would all be better off without me. I truly believed this, as I felt like a broken mess with too much emotional baggage and lack of self-worth. Being desperately tired, I just wanted to sleep to escape that pain. But as I lay on my bed waiting for sleep to come, God spoke to me. He said, 'My child, I will not let you die.' Then I started vomiting and convulsing. Suddenly it hit me what I had done, and I realised with alarming clarity that I didn't want to die. I was too weak to walk, so I crawled out of my bedroom and down the stairs towards our front door. Then I started shouting for help. I collapsed in a heap on the floor and in that moment, I could hear the demons of hell laughing at me. I then passed out.

Fortunately, my friend next door had heard my cries for help and had phoned an ambulance. I have hazy recollections of the paramedics arriving and telling me to stay awake. I tried to do this but kept drifting in and out of consciousness. The last thing I remember was seeing Kevin and my brother just before I was loaded into the ambulance.

I was rushed to the closest hospital and upon arrival I was taken to have my stomach pumped. During this time, I continued to lapse in and out of consciousness, but one thing that I will never forget for as long as I live was the judgement, I received from the nurses who were caring for me. One of them said, 'Can you believe that she's tried to commit suicide when she has two children!' These words seared through my heart, and I was flabbergasted by the judgement and lack of compassion. I was then taken to ICU where I remained for the next twenty-four hours whilst the doctors monitored me.

I remember my dad coming to visit me. He was not a man who was warm or endearing. Instead, all I had known from him was constant criticism and disapproval. I don't remember him ever telling me he loved me or was proud of me. But on this day he visited me in the hospital and thinking I was unconscious; caressed my cheek and told me I had given him a 'terrible scare.' This small gesture meant the world to me as it was the first time my dad had shown any kind of positive emotional response towards me. It's just incredibly sad that it took that set of traumatic events to get him to finally open up and reveal that he did indeed have a heart.

I woke up feeling deeply ashamed of what I had done and the worry I must have caused all my loved ones. But I still felt desperately depressed. I remained in hospital for a week, and I was under the psychiatric care of a doctor who diagnosed me with bipolar II. Although this disorder is not as serious as bipolar I, it is characterised by extreme mood swings, irritability, and depression. I was both relieved and frightened by my diagnosis. On the one hand, I was glad that I could finally put a name to what I had been going through for so many years, but on the flip side of it I was terrified of being branded 'crazy' just like my mother.

I remember falling to my knees one evening just before bed and begging God to take it from me. I cried out to him for his mercy and asked for his forgiveness for trying to take my own life. I was deeply ashamed of what I had done and very embarrassed. In the weeks following my suicide attempt, I learnt a lot about God's grace. He gently lifted me out of my sin and disgrace and held me to his chest where I sobbed deep, gut-wrenching cries from the depths of my being. I was still in so much emotional pain and full of questions, but Jesus was so kind, merciful, and loving and most of all, he didn't judge me. It was during this painful time that the Lord revealed the overwhelming beauty of his character and showed me the father's heart for his hurting child. I was once told that people who commit suicide go straight to hell. Even Christians! But after my experience, I most definitely do not believe this. God showed me he has endless compassion for those who are driven to suicide. He does not condemn them.

In fact, he embraces them and soothes them with his unconditional love.

I was very fragile for several months after my suicide attempt. I didn't know how to return to normal life. Kevin was angry with me over what I had done, which I could fully understand. He felt I had tried to abandon him, and he needed time to heal, too. I diligently took my medication and tried to focus all my energy and focus on my two daughters. It took me about six months to begin to feel human again and really face the world. I felt fractured and broken and even detached from my body – as if the whole experience had happened to someone else. I had no sense of self, and my confidence was shattered. I should have had counselling at that point in my life but for some reason I didn't. I simply tried to get back to my life and adjust to my new normal. Very quickly, I learnt to act OK even when I didn't feel it. The depression was still overwhelming, and I just dealt with it by shoving medication down my throat. I threw myself into my work and tried to focus on raising my two precious daughters, but inside I was dying.

After all the trauma we had suffered because of our psychotic neighbour, we decided to move out of our townhouse in Lonehill and find something else in the area. We felt it would be a new start for us, and we could try to pick up the pieces of our shattered lives.

At this stage, Gabriella was a very active little toddler. She was fiercely independent and had no fear. I went back to freelance graphic design, and we all settled into our new home in another complex in Lonehill.

Chapter Fifteen

Kevin and I tried desperately to find our way back to each other, but by this time so much resentment and heartbreak had built up between us and we simply couldn't connect on a deep level. Looking back on the early years of our marriage, I can now clearly see that Kevin and I were doomed from the start as we both had so much baggage in our lives when we met. I had all the trauma of my childhood, the rape and deep-seated anger towards men because of my critical, alcoholic father.

Kevin had suffered through his parent's divorce and his dad's lack of any real interest in him. So, we both brought filters and wrong thinking and mistrust into the marriage. Also, when I met Kevin, he had just come out of a toxic relationship where he had been betrayed by his girlfriend, so he was nursing a broken heart. I was in the same boat as I had experienced heartbreak when Jonathan had broken up with me and promptly gotten engaged three months later. I took me five years to get over the pain he caused me and the aftermath of the abortion which I bitterly regretted.

We threw ourselves into working hard to carve out a niche for our little family, but Kevin and I had bitter, awful fights where we would throw ugly words at each other. I was so blind to the true character of my kind, long-suffering husband, and all I could see was a man who had betrayed me before we were married, and I fixated on that even though I had done the same thing to him. It really was very hypocritical of me. But despite the emotional turmoil between us, God was faithful, and he became my rock and my shepherd during those painful years.

I felt lonely in a marriage that I had felt pushed into by my family, and resentment swirled around inside me like a dark, ominous mist. In reality, I was so broken and could barely function, but somehow, I made it through those years. I hung onto God and continued to pray for breakthrough and healing of my ailing marriage. I found joy in my darling girls and loved watching them grow. We joined a vibrant, spirit-filled church and gradually life improved. When Rebecca was seven years old, she told me she wanted to give her heart to Jesus and be baptised. This was an incredibly special moment for us, and we celebrated her big decision with a great deal of pride.

After we had been living in our new home in Lonehill for about three years, Kevin and I decided we wanted to leave the rat race of Johannesburg and move slightly out of the city to experience a bit of space and rural living. We found a delightful little cottage on a plot of land about half an hour outside of Johannesburg.

We loved rural living, and I got back into my painting. I had been commissioned by a friend to paint a picture of poppies in oils. I was excited to start and bought a big canvas and stocked up on all my supplies. At the cottage, I converted the spare room into a studio and soon got stuck into my painting.

Even since my suicide attempt, my dad had been a little more doting towards me and phoned me every day. He was still quite critical and bombastic, but looking back now, I can see how God in his grace did a healing work between my dad and I during those years. He even visited the children occasionally and would arrive on our doorstep armed with sweets for the girls. Rebecca was very fond of her granddad and absolutely adored him.

It was around this time that my dad suddenly fell ill. I spoke to him on the phone early one morning and he told me he had been to see the doctor as he had been vomiting for days. The doctor gave him an injection in his right buttock and gave the diagnosis of a stomach disorder. I suspect the injection was not thoroughly sanitised, as a few days later a massive boil erupted on my dad's buttock. He went back to his doctor and was told that he would need to go in for minor surgery to lance the boil.

On the morning of his operation, I received a call from my dad's girlfriend.

'Hi Janine, it's Angie here. I must go to a job interview this morning after I've dropped your dad off at the hospital. Are you able to sit with him whilst he waits for his op?'

'Yes, Angie, I'm happy to do that. All the best for your job interview.'

I added a few more strokes to my painting, which was progressing nicely. I loved the boldness of the red poppies, and it gave me so much joy to express myself creatively again.

I arrived at the hospital and enquired at the nurse's station.

'Hi, I am here to see my dad, Clive Ellis.'

'Oh, yes. He is just down the passage on the left. Room fifteen.'

'Thank you,' I said.

———

When I walked into the room, I could immediately see that my dad was in a great deal of pain. His face was as white as a sheet, and he smiled weakly at me.

I pulled up a chair and reached for his hand. 'How are you feeling, dad?'

'I'm in a lot of pain. Can you ask the nurse for some medication?'

'Yes, of course. I'll be right back.'

I walked out of the hospital room back towards the nurse's station. The same nurse who had helped me earlier was behind the counter. I glanced at her name tag.

'Jennifer, my dad is in a great deal of pain. Is there some medication you could give him to help with it?'

'No, I'm sorry, but he's not allowed any pain medication just before surgery. He is due to go in soon. He'll just have to be patient.'

My shoulders drooped as I made my way back to my dad's room. How on earth would I tell him he's not allowed any pain medication? I could see how much he was suffering.

'Dad, I'm really sorry, but the nurse said you are not allowed any medication as you are just about to go into surgery. It should only be a few more minutes.'

I squeezed his hand and tried to be as reassuring as possible.

'If I can get rid of the pain, I'll never drink again,' my dad said through clenched teeth.

That's when I knew that his pain level was off the charts.

'Hang in there, dad,' I said, hoping that the nurse would arrive soon.

As if on cue, Jennifer walked into the room.

'OK, Mr. Ellis, let's get you into surgery.'

My dad grunted in response, and I got up and leaned forward to kiss him on the cheek.

As he was wheeled away, a sick feeling formed in the pit of my stomach. But I reassured myself that he was simply going in for minor surgery. There was nothing to be concerned about. Little did I know!

I phoned Vaughan to tell him that our dad had gone into surgery.

'Hi Vaughan, dad has gone in now. I'm going to visit him later when he wakes up from the surgery.'

'I don't think that's necessary, Janine. Rather, visit him tomorrow morning as he will probably be grumpy and groggy when he first wakes up.'

A sense of impending doom came over me as I ended the call. I just couldn't seem to shake the feeling that something awful was about to happen. I had been told that the operation would only take an hour, so on my way back to the hospital I popped in to see my mum. Vaughan had kindly built a cottage for her on his property, and she had been living there happily for the past few years.

We shared a cup of tea together and I enjoyed her company. Then I got up to leave.

When I arrived at the hospital, I walked over to the nurse's station.

'Hi, I'm here to see Mr. Ellis. Is he in the recovery ward?'

'We've been trying to reach your family. Mr. Ellis went into cardiac arrest on the operating table.'

I gasped.

'The doctor did CPR, and he is now stable, but in critical

condition. Here is the business card of the surgeon. He wants to speak to you.'

My hand shook as I reached for the card.

I rummaged in my handbag until I felt the outline of my mobile phone. I keyed in the number on the card and waited for the surgeon to answer.

'Hello, Dr Evans, it's Janine Fynn here. I am Mr. Ellis' daughter, and I was asked to phone you.'

'Hi Janine, I'm afraid your dad went into cardiac arrest on the operating table. We managed to do CPR and stabilised him. However, he is a very sick man. He has Fournier's gangrene, which is an acute necrotic infection. I had to cut away a lot of dead flesh. He's in a medically induced coma and is being given adrenaline to keep his heart going. I'm afraid that it's unlikely he'll make it through the night. I am sorry.'

I blinked back the tears welling in my eyes. 'Thank you, doctor.'

Kevin pulled me into an embrace. I felt as if my legs were going to buckle beneath me.

'I need to phone Vaughan,' I said. Kevin nodded.

I waited for my brother to answer his phone.

'Hi boetie, I'm at the hospital and I need you to come here as soon as you can. Dad went into cardiac arrest on the operating table. I've spoken to the surgeon, and he said he is very ill and might not last the night. I'll explain everything when you get here.'

I could hear Vaughan suck in a breath, and I could tell he was struggling to absorb it all.

'Okay, sis. I will be there in a few minutes.'

When my brother arrived, I gave him the biggest hug. I now felt ready to go upstairs to the ICU and see my dad. We approached the doors to the unit with trepidation. My dad had always been larger than life, full of charisma and good humour. It was hard to imagine that he was barely hanging on to his life.

A lump formed in my throat when I saw him lying there, so lifeless and hooked up to a heart machine and ventilator. I walked over to him and took his hand in mine. It felt cold to the touch.

'Dad, I'm here. Please fight this and pull through. I'm not ready to lose you yet.'

A male nurse walked up to us.

'I'm Simon, and I'm looking after the patient.'

'The patient is my dad.'

Irritated, I looked away from Simon and concentrated on my dad. Again, I spoke to him.

'Please dad, don't leave me.'

'You do know he can't hear you,' said Simon. 'He's in a coma.'

The nurse was getting on my already frayed nerves.

'I believe his spirit can hear me, so if you don't mind, I'm going to carry on talking to him.'

My brother was standing on the other side of the hospital bed. His wife Wendy was waiting outside the ICU with Kevin.

'Vaughan, let's pray for dad.'

'Good idea.'

We joined hands and prayed.

'Father God, we come to you now and ask you to please heal our dad. Fill him with your Holy Spirit and help him fight the infection. We pray for a miracle, Lord. Please don't take him until he's had a revelation of who you are, Lord. In Jesus' name, amen.'

Vaughan lived close to the hospital and as it was a long drive out to our cottage on the plot, he suggested that Kevin and I spend the night at his house.

'Come sis, it's getting late. You must be tired. We'll come back and visit him in the morning.'

I nodded and turned to leave. Vaughan and I walked out

together, both silent in our inner thoughts and fears. But faith rose within me, and I continued to pray.

We arrived at Vaughan's house, and we all sat in the lounge discussing my dad over a cup of tea.

We eventually went to bed, but I had a sleepless night. I couldn't get my dad's condition out of my head, and I literally prayed through the night. Knowing my dad wasn't saved, I feared for his soul. I begged God to let him live long enough to make a commitment and give his life to Jesus. I wasn't sure how this was going to happen as he was in a coma, but I held onto the belief that he could hear me.

The following morning, we received a phone call from the hospital to say that my dad had indeed survived the night but was still in a very critical condition. I rejoiced and thanked God for sparing him and we all travelled to the hospital to visit him.

Vaughan and I walked into the ICU, and I was immediately struck by the spiritual atmosphere I experienced when we approached my dad. In my spirit, I could discern that there was a battle going on for my dad's soul. God showed me that Satan was standing in the room waiting to take my dad, but I also saw angels standing guard over him. I looked at his face and noticed that he seemed very troubled. He was frowning, and his eyelids fluttered slightly. I immediately began to pray that my dad would have an encounter with God and that his soul would be saved. I rebuked the enemy and as I prayed, I saw Jesus appear in the room and walk up to my dad. Thanking God for his faithfulness, I noticed that my dad's expression had changed. He now looked peaceful.

I left the ICU and went outside to join Kevin in the waiting room. Whilst I was there, my very dear friend Debbie phoned me. The day before, I had messaged all my friends from church asking them to pray for my dad.

I answered my phone and was immediately comforted by the sound of my friend's voice.

'Do you want me to come to the hospital?' asked Debbie.

'Oh, my friend, I would love that,' I said with tears in my eyes.

'I'm leaving now. I'll see you in fifteen minutes.'

I was grateful beyond words. Debbie was a real prayer warrior and an amazing woman of God, and I was looking forward to seeing her. I had met her at our local church, and she had impressed me with her warmth and genuine friendship. I loved her deeply and was so incredibly grateful that she was prepared to come to the hospital.

When Debbie arrived, I gave her the biggest hug, and had to swallow hard to stop myself from falling apart right there in the hospital. We walked over to the waiting room chairs and sat down facing each other. She looked at me with so much compassion in her eyes.

'Is your dad saved?' she asked.

'I don't know. I don't think so.'

'Well, I believe there are deaf and dumb people in heaven who couldn't speak to make a commitment and the same applies to your dad. You go in there and say the sinner's prayer to him.'

'That's a really good idea,' I said. 'The nurse keeps telling me that my dad can't hear me as he's in a coma, but I believe he can. Thanks for your advice, Debbie. You are a true friend. I'm going to do that right now.'

I got up and walked back to the ICU. I approached my dad with a sick feeling in the pit of my stomach. It was just so heart-breaking to see him hooked up to so many machines. I pulled up a chair next to him and spoke gently to him.

'Dad, I believe you can hear me. I also believe that God has answered my prayers, and you have had an encounter with Jesus.

I'd like you to say the sinner's prayer after me and agree with me in your spirit. God will hear your heart's cry and will save you.'

I said the sinner's prayer and immediately a feeling of peace settled over me like a warm blanket. I knew in my heart that my dad had accepted Jesus. As I continued to pray for him, God told me it was time to let him go. He said that my dad was holding on as he didn't want to let me down, but in fact he wanted to go as he had seen heaven. It was one of the hardest decisions I have ever made, but I knew it was the right one. I stroked my dad's face and swallowed past the tears.

'Dad, it's okay, you can let go now. God has shown me you've had a glimpse of heaven and you want to go there. So, go with my blessing and I'll see you again one day. I love you.'

My whole body ached from the tension I had been feeling for the past twenty-four hours. I was also dog tired from not having sleep at all the night before. I squeezed my dad's hand and then left the ICU.

On the drive to my brother's house, the strangest thing happened. Kevin and I witnessed a car racing past us and then hitting a pedestrian who was trying to cross the road. He was flung high into the air and then hit the road. Kevin immediately stopped the car and got out to assist the man. The car had already sped off, and the driver had not even stopped. I was appalled. We saw a miracle that night as when Kevin reached the man, he saw that not only was he alive, but he got up onto his feet and disappeared into the darkness!

Both Kevin and I had a strong sense that God had taken my dad home at the exact moment that the car hit the man, and he had decided to spare the life of the unfortunate man. It was a bizarre feeling.

We arrived at Vaughan's house, and we had only been there for about ten minutes when the phone rang. Vaughan got up to answer it, but we all knew it was the hospital.

Vaughan walked into the lounge. His eyes were red-rimmed and bloodshot. He blinked back the tears.

'Dad's gone.'

I nodded and then went to sit next to him on the couch. I put my arm around his shoulders, and I had a feeling of gratitude that we could all be together at such a sad time.

The next few days were spent planning a memorial for my dad. I said to Vaughan that dad would have wanted us to celebrate his life and we needed to also rejoice that he was now in heaven. On the day of the memorial, I dressed my two little girls in beautiful white dresses with a rosebud trim and I wore a light green suit. I encouraged those attending the memorial to dress in bright, happy colours and to avoid the usual somber black clothing. I knew my dad would have hated that.

I got up to say a few words, and I told the congregation that my dad had found peace at the end, which I'm sure comforted those who knew and loved him.

After the memorial, life continued, but I struggled in my grief. I felt as if there was a massive hole inside of me and although my relationship with my dad was complicated, I missed him terribly. I felt cheated that he had lost his life tragically at the age of sixty-seven. But even in my grief, God was tender and kind, and he constantly reminded me that my dad was with him and that should he have lived, his life would have been terrible. The surgeon had said that he would need multiple operations to remove dead flesh because of the impact of the Fournier's gangrene.

God in his mercy had taken my dad, and much as I missed him, I was grateful for that.

As my dad had been cremated, Vaughan and I discussed where we should sprinkle his ashes. My dad loved Lake Kariba in Zimbabwe and would often hire a houseboat to go on three-day long drinking and fishing sprees with his good friends. So, we contacted his friends and arranged to go out on a houseboat and sprinkle my dad's ashes at sundown.

Once it was all arranged, a few months later, Vaughan and I flew to Zimbabwe. We then drove with my dad's friends from Harare (the city) to Kariba where a houseboat was waiting for us. There were two of my dad's friends on the houseboat with us, as well as a cook. We spent three days on the boat enjoying the magnificent scenery and wildlife. On our last evening there, we rowed out to Antelope Island at sundown. The sky was breathtaking. We said a prayer and sprinkled my dad's ashes across the lake. Then I read a poem. Vaughan poured a whiskey (my dad's favourite drink) and then we toasted him and poured the whiskey into the lake too. We felt it was a fitting farewell and something that my dad would have appreciated. I found it cathartic, and it gave me a sense of closure.

Chapter Sixteen

Around this time, Kevin and I started to discuss the option of moving to Cape Town. Johannesburg was riddled with crime, and we had endured so many terrible experiences there. We had heard that the crime rate in Cape Town was not nearly as bad, and we felt we could give our girls a better lifestyle by the coast. We prayed about the decision, and we felt God was giving us the green light to go. We were desperate to leave crime-ridden Johannesburg and we were prepared to take a leap of faith.

We managed to secure a rental in Durbanville, which is in the northern suburbs of Cape Town. So, we packed up and left. We were all looking forward to leaving all our trauma behind and starting a new life in Cape Town.

We didn't have jobs to go to and we arrived with just our belongings and a relatively small sum of money to survive on. But God was good to us and within a couple of months, both Kevin and I secured jobs. My sister Leigh also lived in Durbanville, and she was a tremendous help when we first arrived in Cape Town. I enrolled our girls in a lovely Christian school just down the road from where we lived. We settled into our new lives, and whenever we had the chance, we visited the beach. The girls adapted well and made friends at their new school.

I really enjoyed my new job and got on well with my boss. Within six months, I was promoted from Marketing Assistant to New Media Manager. I was rewarded with a lovely office overlooking a pond with ducks and other birds. But the job itself was challenging, as there was a lot of office politics to navigate. I worked with some difficult individuals, which inspired me to write this poem.

Corporate Fools

The corporate fools like sheep in a wolf's clothing.
baying for blood; they disguise their loathing.
Each rung of the ladder on their brother's back,
Doing so well, promoted ahead of the pack.

The cards are stacked in their favour or so it seems,
the tower of cards will crash and fall in their dreams.
They scheme and strategise as they straighten their ties.
Their days are numbered, but how the time flies.

They have sold their souls for the pursuit of pleasure.
Never mind their conscience, they believe they're clever.
Thick skinned as heavy Rhinos and shrewd as snakes.
Their swarmy limp handshakes and smiles are fakes.

From the goblet of greed, they have already sipped,
Over littered bodies they've shamed but never tripped.
Their hearts are black, and their souls are dead.
The hunger that aches in their bellies needs more bread.

They drive in cars that make them feel smart.

But they're foolish and dull without much heart.
Time so fleeting will take all they took and did not give.
As empty and broke they'll enter a cold barren grave.

Kevin also enjoyed working for a retail fit out company and for a while our lives were relatively uneventful.

After living in a small three bedroomed cottage, we decided after a couple of years that we needed more space. We looked around for another property and were thrilled to find a larger house just five minutes down the road from where we were staying. It was four bedroomed with two living areas and was positioned in a gated, safe complex. I turned the fourth, downstairs bedroom into a studio and for the first year, we were very happy there. At that stage, little did we know our lives were going to be turned upside down by a sequence of events.

In the winter of that year, Rebecca developed mumps. I could not take time off work to care for her, so I left her with Rosie, our maid, with strict instructions to make sure she ate well and got lots of rest. She seemed to recover from mumps and went back to school, but a couple of days later, I received a phone call from the school saying Rebecca was vomiting. I made excuses to my boss and raced back to Durbanville from Somerset West. Rebecca told me she was feeling very thirsty, and I noticed she had lost an alarming amount of weight in the past twenty-four hours!

I rushed her to the doctor, and the prognosis was suspected pancreatitis. Apparently, in rare cases, mumps can develop into this life-threatening condition. I was advised to take Rebecca for an abdominal scan at the local hospital.

As Rebecca's pancreas was not enlarged in the scan, pancreatitis was ruled out and I took her home. But she continued to get worse and could barely stand, so I took her back to my GP. It was then that my GP took a urine sample and then told me I needed to see my pediatrician urgently. When we arrived there,

Dr Fourie took a urine sample and then told me I needed to rush Rebecca to ICU as she had a very high blood glucose reading and was in an acute state of ketoacidosis. He couldn't understand how she was still standing, as normally a blood glucose reading of forty-eight resulted in a coma and even death. When he told me the diagnosis of type 1 insulin-dependent diabetes, the bottom of my world fell out.

I was really frightened but determined to remain strong and calm for Rebecca's sake. Dr Fourie had phoned ahead so that when we arrived at ICU, she was admitted right away and put onto a drip filled with medication to reverse the ketoacidosis.

Once she was settled, I went down to reception to complete all the paperwork. After I had done that, I sent text messages to all my church friends explaining what was going on. I asked them all to pray, as Rebecca was not out of danger yet. I was terrified of losing her and I phoned Kevin, who was working in Durban at the time.

'Hi love, I'm afraid I have some bad news about Rebecca.'

'What's wrong—is she okay?'

'She's been diagnosed with type 1 diabetes, and she has ketoacidosis which is because her blood glucose reading was off the charts. I had to rush her to ICU. She's on a drip and stable. But she's not out of the woods. The next twenty-four hours will be telling.'

'Oh no, I can't believe it! I'll try to get a flight out tonight. I'll do that now and get back to you. Please tell Rebecca that I love her.'

'Yes, I will. Speak to you later.'

I went back to ICU and sat down on the chair next to Rebecca's bed. She looked so tiny in the great big bed, and she was as white as a ghost with dark rings under her eyes. I still couldn't believe how much weight had literally dropped off her over the past twenty-four hours.

I held her hand and prayed for her, trying hard to silence my pounding heart that seemed to reverberate in my ears.

A little later, I received a text message from Kevin saying that there were no flights that evening, but he had managed to get on one first thing the following morning. I was so relieved that he would be joining me the next day.

I phoned my sister Leigh and asked if Gabriella could spend the night with her as I would be staying at the hospital. She agreed so that was at least one less thing to worry about.

Around 8 p.m., one of the nurses brought a pillow and a blanket. She looked at me with compassion in her eyes.

'Mrs. Fynn, would you like me to bring you a cup of tea?'

I immediately warmed to the nurse. I looked at the tag on her uniform. 'Thank you, Karen, I would love that. But please call me Janine.' Karen nodded and then turned to walk away.

I spent a very restless night crammed into the La-Z-Boy chair. I had tiny pockets of sleep, but most of the time I lay awake praying for my darling child.

The following morning, Kevin arriving carrying an adorable teddy bear. Rebecca was delighted to see him, and I noticed she was looking better. The dark half-moons under her eyes had gone and she was feeling hungry.

As if on cue, Dr Fourie arrived. He had such a friendly and caring bedside manner, and I immediately warmed to him. He seemed less stressed that the evening before.

'Mr. and Mrs. Fynn, we have been successful in reversing the ketoacidosis, and Rebecca's blood sugar levels have dropped considerably. As she is now a type 1 diabetic, she will need to test her blood every two to three hours and she will have to take insulin according to her reading every time she eats something. I have arranged for a dietician to come and speak to you all about carbohydrate counting and a representative will also pop in to give you a free testing machine. She should be here any minute. In the meantime, the nurse will do a test on Rebecca to establish her blood glucose level before she can go ahead and eat breakfast.'

I was speechless. How could this have happened to my precious little girl? She was only nine years old. And she was so brave. She hadn't complained once. I reached for her little hand resting on the blanket.

'We'll get through this, my baby. I'm right here with you, OK? I will be your wingman.'

Rebecca smiled at me. 'Thanks, mama. I love you.'

'Love you too, my angel.' My eyes burned with the threat of tears, but I was determined to stay strong for Rebecca. She needed me now, more than ever.

The nurse arrived with the testing machine and pricked Rebecca's finger, instructing her as she went along. She then inserted the blood-soaked testing strip into the machine and waited for it to display her blood glucose reading. It was fifteen, which is still higher than it should be. The nurse then showed her how to select the units of insulin required and how to inject the insulin into key places on her body, such as her abdomen or arm.

I was in awe of my child. She was incredibly strong and told me that next time she wanted to do the test and the injection herself.

Rebecca's breakfast arrived, and I was relieved to see her tuck into it. She hadn't eaten the night before, so I could understand just how hungry she was.

I sat down on the La-Z-Boy and picked up my laptop. As I was the New Media Manager for my company, I oversaw updating the website daily. I did what I needed to do whilst the medical representative went through the procedure with Rebecca.

A Mum's Prayer

I didn't know my heart could burst with love.
For my beautiful child, an angel from above.
But the anguish consumes as I hear her cries.
her brave smile hiding a thin, sad disguise.

Diabetes has gripped her and shattered her dreams,
I'm not sure she fully understands what it means.
As she lies in the hospital bed, pale and still.
I am awed by her courage and iron will.

She's my precious child, my heart's delight,
And I am frightened by her dreaded plight.
Her tears start to fall, and I hold her close,
as she carefully injects her daily dose.

I whisper a prayer as I feel God is nearby.
His love abounds so I need not fear.
I kiss my child and stroke her face.
enfolding her in my tender embrace.

Chapter Seventeen

As a family, we were all shell-shocked by Rebecca's diagnosis of type 1 diabetes. When she came home from the hospital, we all tried to adjust to our new reality. As Rebecca's blood glucose level needed to be tested every two hours, we realised that I would have to give up my job to care for her. We prayed about what to do. Kevin applied for a job in Ghana, which was very well paid and would make up the forty percent deficit in our income when I resigned from my job.

Kevin got the job, but it meant that he would be away working in Ghana for twelve weeks and then he would be home for a week. I knew it would be incredibly tough, but we felt that this was the only open door for us. I reluctantly agreed, and I resigned from my job.

Adjusting to the diabetes was incredibly hard. Rebecca was very resilient and insisted on doing all her own testing and injections. I was blown away by her bravery. She went back to school and settled into her routine as best she could. But during those early months, we had a couple of scares where her blood sugar levels dropped dangerously low, and she collapsed. Fortunately, I got her to eat some glucose and she recovered within a few minutes. I found it all terrifying, and I spent many nights crying into my pillow, asking God how he could have allowed this awful disease to come upon my precious little girl. God never answered my question, but he did continually tell me that his grace is sufficient.

To keep my sanity intact, I joined our local gym and started attending every morning whilst Rebecca was at school. I had written a detailed letter to her teacher with strict instructions regarding the diabetes and has also met with her in person to discuss the way forward. She was very supportive and that at least gave me a measure of peace of mind. Still, it didn't stop me worrying about my child whilst she was apart from me. To be honest, I found it incredibly difficult, but we muddled our way through those first few months.

When I visited the gym, I decided to join the Zumba dance classes which was a tonic for my soul. Not only was it loads of fun, but I met an awesome bunch of women who became my lifeline during the year Kevin was away working in Ghana. I became especially close to Ruth, who was a laugh a minute and kept my spirits up even on the darkest of days. She stood by me and encouraged me in the most beautiful, kind, and caring way. To this day, she is still one of my best friends and I am so grateful for her. Looking back, I can see God's hand on my life, even though I felt like a single mum. He sent me angels to walk beside me and, most of all, to make me laugh. It became a routine to meet at the gym, attend a Zumba class and then catch up over coffee afterwards. I honestly feel that the combination of the exercise and the company of all those lovely women was a tonic for my soul, which prevented me from falling into the depths of despair.

But it was also a desperately lonely time for me. When I went to bed at night after putting my two girls to bed, I would cry into my pillow, just wishing that the diabetes had never happened. To compound my situation, I missed Kevin and his support. I found it hard to come to terms with the fact that we didn't have an option but for him to go to Ghana.

There was much excitement in the household after the first twelve weeks were up and Kevin came home for a week. He arrived armed with all sorts of exotic gifts, such as shell necklaces and beadwork. He had so many stories to tell us about the lovely locals in Ghana. Kevin told us it was a very Christian nation, and the people were warm and friendly. As it was on the coast, fishing was a big event attended by many locals and even Kevin occasionally. He showed us photographs of the sharks he had caught and the fun he had. It warmed my heart that he was meeting wonderful people and enjoying some down time occasionally. But of course, we spoke about how difficult it was for us as a couple, as we had to adjust to each other all over again once he was home. After the week ended, he returned to Ghana and the girls, and I carried on with our lives.

During that year, I drew very close to God, and he was my lifeline and the lifter of my head. On so many occasions, I lost it and dissolved into tears behind closed doors. But always, my Saviour was there to pick me up off the floor and remind me he was with me, and I was not alone. I found the diabetes very difficult to control and Rebecca's blood sugar levels were up and down and all over the place. There was always a bountiful number of sweets and treats at her school brought in by her friends. As a nine-year-old child, it was very difficult for her to turn down the offers, so she ate them in secret and then injected insulin to compensate. Then tearfully she would confess to me she had secretly eaten sweets. She had a little booklet where she had to record all her blood sugar readings and I would check it every day. So, when her readings were high, I would question her about it. But when she dissolved into tears, I would embrace her and tell her it was all OK and that I understood. But inside, my heart was breaking into a million pieces, wishing I could take the diabetes into my own body so that she didn't have to suffer. I felt so helpless and every day I would cry out to God, begging him to heal my daughter. I firmly believed that God could do this, but during that time I also learnt that, for some reason, not known to me, God sometimes chooses not to heal. This is one of the great mysteries this side of heaven. I think we will only find out the answer once we enter eternity.

Chapter Eighteen

The years flew by and eventually, once I felt Rebecca was old enough to cope with the diabetes on her own, I went back to work full time. Even so, I worried about her constantly and the transition back to work was not an easy one.

I secured a copywriting job at MiX Telematics in Stellenbosch. The minute I arrived at work on my first day, I just knew that I was going to love working there. My boss and my peers were so lovely, and I immediately felt welcome. I settled in and thoroughly enjoyed my work. I worked on creative concepts, which were right up my street.

After a couple of years working at MiX Telematics, Kevin and I began to discuss the option of moving back to the UK so that our girls would have a better future. The cost of living in South Africa was very high and the crime rate was spiraling out of control. Every day there were news reports about farmers who had been murdered and although we loved South Africa, we felt that a move was inevitable.

The more Kevin and I discussed it, the more certain we

became. It was the right step. We prayed about it and asked God to make a way for a smooth transition.

On the 5th of September 2015, we arrived in the UK. It was a leap of faith as Kevin and I didn't have jobs to come to and to add to it, Kevin could only get into the UK on a visitor's visa. I had a British passport, as did Rebecca. We stayed in a lovely little cottage in Kent for the first few weeks and I got to work looking for a job. I also enrolled the girls in local schools, and we began our new lives in the UK. We were relieved to be away from all the crime in South Africa, but even so, it was a difficult transition. The girls missed the South African sunshine, the beaches, mountains and, of course, their friends.

I settled into my new job, and Kevin returned to South Africa to run his business there. For the immediate future, he would have to come back to the UK every few months as that was all his visitor's visa allowed. Because of this, the first two years in the UK were incredibly hard as I felt like a single mum again. I was working all day and then coming home to two very disgruntled daughters who were battling to adjust to their new normal. They were both being bullied at school, and they were just miserable. I felt thinly spread and, looking back now, I can honestly say that God carried me through those early years in the UK. Eventually, Kevin secured a visa which would allow him to live and work in the UK and finally he moved over for good. He closed his business in South Africa and was excited to start a new life in the UK.

It was such a relief having him with me. He secured a job at BMR Construction, but it was a big adjustment for him. Kevin hated the winter months and, like me and the girls, desperately missed the temperate climate of Cape Town. Having lived in the UK before, Kevin and I knew it would take a few years for our girls to settle in, but even so, we didn't for a minute think it would be quite as hard as it was! For the first few years, we limped along trying hard to settle in, but we were all dreadfully home-sick. We moved to Sevenoaks and joined a wonderful church, which made a difference. Slowly, we made friends and even connected with other South Africans in the area. Despite the difficulties of adjusting to a new and very different culture, the girls did well at school and Rebecca graduated from high school with her GCSEs. The following year, she went to West Kent College to study fashion design, something she was passionate about. During this time, I was very worried about Gabriella. She was so unhappy and struggling with being bullied at school. I spoke to her about moving schools, but she was adamant that it would make no difference and that she would probably get bullied at another school too. I phoned the teachers and spoke to the headmaster, and they said they would keep an eye on her. But it did little to ease my concern. Eventually, after a couple of years, she finished her GCSEs and left that awful school.

Rebecca excelled in her fashion design course and achieved a distinction at the end of the two-year term. For her final project, she was asked to design an ocean-inspired garment. Her dress was so well thought out that it was chosen as the finale garment at the West Kent College Fashion Show. It was very exciting to attend the fashion show and see the model wearing Rebecca's dress. It was a very special time, and Kevin and I were immensely proud of both of our girls.

I then enrolled Gabriella into West Kent College to do her A levels as she wanted to go to university and study law. She chose three subjects for her A levels: Law, Sociology and Business Studies. Gabriella is a very studious child, and she worked very hard to achieve the grades she was hoping for. She settled well into the college and met her first boyfriend there. James is a kind, thoughtful, polite, and caring young man who has been instrumental in helping her adjust to the British way of life. The young couple are very much in love and Gabriella feels she has met her soulmate. They have now been together for almost two years and Gabriella is much happier in the UK.

Chapter Nineteen

We have now been in the UK for almost seven years. Although it has been hard, I can look back and see God's hand on our family. He has always been there to lead and guide us. Four months ago, I started a new job where, because of the COVID pandemic, which has been raging for the past two years, I am able to work from home most of the week. It is mandatory to go into the office twice a week on Mondays and Wednesdays.

God is so good, as I had prayed for a job that I would enjoy. I also asked for a job that would not be too far away. The office is in Crawley, which is a half hour's drive away from Sevenoaks. I also love the work as it's copywriting for a company called B&CE. The company is very good to its employees and not only supports the staff with training and career progression, but also offers annual performance-based bonuses.

Kevin is doing well working for himself as an independent contractor. Again, God has answered our prayers as his last contract ended a few weeks ago and so we were seeking God for the next step. I asked the Lord for three things. First, that Kevin would find work close to where we lived as many of his projects had taken him far away from home and he could only get back on the weekends. Second, I asked God for a project that Kevin would enjoy as his last project was not in the field that he most wanted to work in. Third, I asked for good pay.

Just a week ago, all my prayers were answered. Kevin secured a contract in Biggin Hill, which is a mere twenty-minute drive from our home. It is a site management role where he oversees a hotel build which he really enjoys, having worked on The Marriott Hotel in Ghana all those years ago.

As I look back over my life, I am overwhelmed by God's grace, mercy, and unfailing love. I have made mistakes and fallen back into sin time and time again. But always God has gently picked me up, dusted me off and showed me the way to go. Recently, I realised I needed to be set free from all the traumatic memories from my childhood. For years I had just shut it all down and carried on regardless, but inside there was a huge, festering wound that was crippling me. I had rejection and aban-donment issues, and I didn't want to carry these around with me anymore. I sought Christian counselling and was thrilled when my church referred me to a lovely lady, Carol. She was also a Christian and spent most of her time helping others through prayer and counselling.

The first time I met Carol, I was moved by her warmth and compassion. She is a lady in her seventies who has suffered much loss and heartbreak during her life, and I immediately felt an affinity with her. She set a date for me to receive counselling with her and when the day dawned, I couldn't wait to start.

I told Carol all about my mum's mental illness and my traumatic childhood. She just listened and then said to me that she thought I was one of the bravest woman she had ever met. These words just moved me to tears. Finally, I had found someone who truly understood my suffering. She prayed for me and asked me to go back to the small wooden hut in the garden of my grandmother's house where Leigh and I had prayed. My prayer had been, *please God, don't take my mum away*. And still, as I mentioned earlier in the book, an ambulance came and took her away. Carol asked me to imagine Jesus with me there in that little hut and then prayed for the healing of my emotions. She also asked me to describe what I was feeling at the time. It was incredibly cathartic to talk about it, and once she had prayed for me, I felt an incredible release.

Weary Pilgrim
Weary pilgrim through life's barren land,
Roadmap of truth clutched in calloused hand.
His back to the wind, the sun on his face,
Though perils abound and the way is steep,
his step is chartered even unto the deep.
Demons may growl from pits beneath,
his heart unto death to him is bequeathed.
No surety of step, no escape from pain,
but a quiet peace is his one sure gain.
His compass knowledge of the One who calls,
and in whose radiance all else palls.

It was around this time that God started talking to me about butterflies. He showed me that for most of my life, I had been in a cocoon of pain, but I was not alone in it. Whilst I was in that dark night of the soul, he was working in me. He also showed me how much I had struggled with self-loathing. For years, I had an identity crisis and despised who I was. I had made so many mistakes in my life and I honestly didn't trust myself.

But God has now changed all of that. During this past year, he has gently shown me which wounds need healing. It never ceases to amaze me just how kind and tender he is. God gives us free will to make our own decisions, which is amazing, but the best part is that even when we go astray and make mistakes, he always forgives us if we repent. His mercy knows no bounds, and he wants nothing more than for us all to live an abundant life free of past hurt. Jesus died on the cross and took all our pain upon him. This fact never ceases to amaze me. The gift of eternal life if we turn to him is free and when I finally truly got this, I just wanted to shout it from the rooftops. I wrote a poem called *The Emperor's Sword* to describe this.

The Emperor's Sword

I am my Emperor's sword,
divinely commissioned
by my sovereign Lord.
I'll not be sheathed until I die,
'His kingdom come' will be my heart's cry.

I'll not surrender 'til the victory bell tolls,
The harvest is white with so many lost souls.
I'll wear His banner; I'll shout His name.
Until all near and far, have heard of His fame.

I'll bend but not break, grow weary but not faint.
Until He shines like the sun, in the mirror of His saint.
And when at last my zealous race is run,
I'll be sheathed by the hand of the Emperor's Son.

If you are reading this and you don't yet know Jesus, I want to encourage you to turn to him. We are living in such troubling times and everything that is happening in the world today has been prophesied in the Bible. We are living in the end days and Jesus will soon return to take his people home. What a glorious day that will be!

There are many people out there trapped in cocoons of fear because of the state of the world. If you are one of those people, I want to urge you that you too can find freedom. If you accept Jesus into your life, he will work in you whilst you are in that cocoon and when the time is right, he will gently draw you out of the cocoon and put you onto a branch where you can sit as your wings dry. The beauty of the butterfly is proof that you can go through a great deal of darkness and still become something beautiful. This is one of the great wonders of God, and I am living testimony of that. I can now honestly say that I am completely healed and set free from my past. I no longer struggle with crippling depression and anxiety and God has dried my wings and now I can fly.

I want to urge all of you in cocoons to be encouraged by my story. You may have been in a cocoon for many years and might be despairing that you will ever be set free from it. But I want to say to you, WAIT! I can't tell you when God will decide to draw you out of your cocoon, but I can emphatically say to you that in his perfect time, he WILL do it. He has engraved your name on the palm of his hand, so how could he possibly forget about you?

The incredible thing is that he knew you before he created the earth. You have been on his mind since before time began. Isn't that just the most incredible fact?

I can testify to God's goodness. I was in the cocoon for over fifty years. There's a scripture in the Bible that says, *hope deferred makes the heart sick.* Well, I certainly had a sick heart! I despaired that God had forgotten me and that he would never come and set me free. But he did! Yes, it took many years, and I was tested to the limit, and I made many mistakes, but God pursued me. He is the good shepherd who will leave his ninety-nine sheep to find that one lost sheep. Then he will carry it gently on his shoulders and take it back to the flock. Isn't that just so amazing? His eyes are always on us and he doesn't leave us, not for a second!

Since the Lord has healed me and set me free from the cocoon, he has continued to talk to me about the metamorphosis phase. He has also told me that there are many broken women who are still trapped in cocoons. It could be the cocoon of a hard marriage, or the cocoon of sickness. Perhaps you are terminally ill? It could be the cocoon of financial worries. Just know that wherever you are at, God will meet you. He will never forsake you or leave you. He is good, and he wants you to spend eternity with him. But he also wants you to experience the freedom of being a beautiful butterfly. He wants you to be free in every area of your life. He wants you to experience his kingdom here on earth.

If you are currently in a cocoon, I want to tell you to persevere. Your freedom could come as soon as today or tomorrow. I also want you to know that nothing, and I mean absolutely nothing, you go through in life is worthless. Every pain you have ever felt is also experienced by our Saviour. He collects our tears in a bottle and he sees every time you have been rejected, betrayed, lied to, or hurt in any way. And the beauty of it all is that he works everything together for good. Nothing you have gone through is wasted. Perhaps you have gone through betrayal and can now help other women who have suffered the same fate.

Perhaps you've suffered years of illness, and now you can encourage others in the same predicament.

My prayer is that as you have read my story, you have been drawn to our wonderful Creator. I hope you have heard him whisper to your heart in the pages of this book. My desire is for you to know him as I do. May you too have a powerful testimony to his goodness and mercy. I also want to encourage you to *not grow weary in well doing for in due season you will reap the reward.* This scripture is close to my heart, as God has given it to me many times over the years when I despaired that anything would change.

If you're in a cocoon, may you be set free to fly as a beautiful butterfly on the gentle thermals of the wind. Your time is coming! Just believe and embrace it.

Chapter Twenty

Throughout my life, I have wrestled with the age-old question why does a good God allow so much suffering in the world? In my own limited capacity, I have come up with an answer to that difficult question. We live in a fallen world and because Satan has dominion over the earth suffering, disease and all manner of awful calamities abound. God never ever wanted us to suffer but he has also given us free choice. Sometimes we suffer because of wrong decisions we have made (like my decision to have an abortion).

But what I find incredible about God is his limitless grace. When I finally grasped that he had truly forgiven me for what I had done, I was moved deeply. Repeatedly, throughout my life God has shown me grace and mercy and for that I will be forever grateful.

Maybe there's a sin in your life that you feel is too ugly or too big for you to be forgiven. I want to encourage you that Jesus died on the cross for that sin, and nothing is too big for him to not forgive it. The case in point here is when Jesus was dying on the cross, the murderer next to him asked for mercy and Jesus graciously gave it and the man received eternal life. Isn't that just the most amazing act of compassion and love? He didn't judge the murderer, but simply embraced him instead. Then he said, 'today you will be with me in paradise.' How beautiful!

I've made a lot of mistakes in my life, and I have walked away from God time and time again, but as you can see by my journey, he never gave up on me. He relentlessly pursued me and when I came back to him, he embraced me and forgave me. As I walk with him and learn more about his unconditional love, I am forever changed. Just like that caterpillar in the chrysalis, I have been transformed by God's redeeming power. That of course doesn't mean that I don't have my bad days and I am sin free. No, I wrestle with sin just like everybody else, but in Christ I can overcome the desire to sin, and I can walk victoriously.

Recently, God has been talking to me about knowing my identity in him. During my quiet time a few weeks ago, God said to me, 'Do you know that you are a warrior princess of the most high God – the King?' I said yes, I do know that, but I haven't been living it. If we can truly grasp that we are warriors who can overcome any trial, tribulation, or sin then we have a hope of living truly transformed lives. The world judges Christians very harshly as those who don't know the Lord look at our defeated lack-luster lives and ask themselves where is their joy, where is their peace, where is their victory? Then they conclude that Christianity has no power, and they casually discard it on the garbage pile along with all their other haughty assumptions and opinions.

We need to experience more breakthrough and victory in our lives. God has given us the tools to do this. The next time the enemy lies to you about who you are and points out the sin in your life, remind him that you are a warrior of the King and fear has no place in you.

Because I had such a traumatic childhood, fear was never far from me. I can honestly say that I struggled with gut wrenching, crippling fear, and anxiety for most of my life. It was only about a year ago that I was delivered of this, but it required a lot of work on my part. God showed me that I am indeed a warrior, and I can fight the fiery darts of the devil, by proclaiming the Word of God over my situation. I would do this aloud and keep doing it until I could feel the fear lose its grip on me. Psalm 91 is my favourite warfare psalm in the Bible. Often when I've been afraid, I've recited the psalm out loud and declared it to the heavens and the earth and immediately the tension leaves my body and is replaced by peace.

The enemy is relentless, and he doesn't give up easily. You must keep wielding your sword and quoting scriptures that testify that you are an overcomer. Jesus did not die in vain, he died to set you free from the tactics of the devil and it's up to you to claim that victory in your everyday life.

I've also wrestled with the diagnosis of bipolar II that I received many years ago. At first, I was angry and frustrated and in fact very afraid of the stigmatism of this label. All my life, I have watched my mum suffer through people's judgement of her mental illness. When I received that diagnosis, I was so afraid that I would be labelled crazy or looney. I didn't want to turn out just like my mum. But God has been very gracious, and he has helped me to overcome my fears. He has reminded me that I am nothing like my mother and in fact I am the most stable now than I've ever been. This is due to a few factors such as God's healing, counselling and finally medication that works. One of the symptoms of bipolar II is extreme irritability and mood swings. Before I was put on the right medication, I would swing from high to low several times in one day! My poor, long-suffering husband had a lot to cope with (as did my children) and for years I was very difficult to live with.

Because of my tumultuous childhood, the rape and other hurts that entered my life in my early twenties, I was also a very angry person. This was also tough on my family as I would trigger at the slightest provocation and erupt like a volcano. But God has been good, and I can honestly say that I haven't had a single angry outburst in the past couple of years. He had taken that deep rooted anger and fear and replaced it with his wonderful peace and assurance. It's a huge relief for me to be even-tempered and stable. I have yearned for this for many years and finally I am experiencing it.

I want to expound a little more on mental illness. As it has greatly impacted my life, I want to just reiterate how important it is to have grace and compassion for someone who is suffering with a mental disorder. In modern day society the numbers of depressed people are growing by the day. And the suicide levels are off the charts. There is less stigmatism now than there used to be, but I find in general people are still scared of mental illness and definitely shy away from speaking about it.

God had to do a radical work in my heart in order for me to write my memoir and openly talk about my own mental illness. This has been several years in the making. Even today, not many people in my life know about my struggles. Only my very close family and friends know that I have bipolar disorder. So, for me to go public with this knowledge has been a big step for me. But I have chosen to do it in the hope that my story encourages and inspires others out there who are afflicted with mental illness. If this is you, I want to remind you that Jesus knows your pain and he sees your struggles. If you allow him to, he will lift you out of the dark pit and put your feet on the rock. This is not to say you won't sometimes have bad days. You will. These happen to the best of us. But, if you turn to him and choose to walk with him, he will heal and restore you.

I truly believe that the day will come when I won't be dependent on medication to handle the mental illness. I want to be free of it more than anything. I believe that is God's will for me just like I believe he wants to heal my daughter of the diabetes. That takes me into a whole other, very contentious issue about healing. But I might as well dive right in as it needs to be spoken about.

This is a topic that I have acutely wrestled with during my lifetime and most especially when Rebecca was diagnosed with diabetes. For years I have begged God to heal her, and I have held on in faith and believed that he could and would heal her. I've also prayed for healing of my own mental health issues and the crippling headaches that I live with every day, but still, he remains silent. So, what do we do when we don't hear from God and our hearts are desperate for answers? We stand on the promises in the Word of God. One of my favourite scriptures brings me comfort every time I read it. *Know the plans I have for you. Plans to prosper you and not to harm you. Plans to give you a hope and a future.'* Isn't this just the most amazing promise? We have hope in a good God who wants to give us the most wonderful future. There is no need to fear as he has it all under control. Even when he is silent, he is working for our good.

For some reason unknown to me this side of eternity, God doesn't always heal. Yes, he can and does heal and I have seen the evidence with my own eyes, but sometimes he chooses not to heal. Why does he do this?

Well, I believe that it is for his glory. I was chatting the other day to a dear friend about the 'sweet spot' I have experienced with God in my suffering. I think many Christians who have suffered greatly both physically and emotionally have found this place. It is where God becomes more real and there is a deeper level of intimacy and peace that is experienced in that sweet spot. I believe that when a Christian has resigned to the fact that healing is not happening but still trusts God and doesn't turn away from him, this brings him glory. I also believe that God uses our present sufferings and ailments to mold our character into the image of Christ, which in turn produces more fruit in our lives.

There is nothing more beautiful in my humble opinion than a Christian who has made peace with their suffering and in so doing displays the glory of God. When the Lord first started talking to me about butterflies and the metamorphosis period, he told me that it's important to remember that the butterfly's beautiful colours are not for itself. Instead, these colours are to be enjoyed by all the spectators who are watching that beautiful butterfly take its first flight. That butterfly cannot see its wings. And this is how God is with us. He draws us out of that cocoon and then gently puts us on a branch as we wait for our wings to dry.

We may have emerged from that cocoon still carrying an illness or emotional burden, but he knows that our character has been molded whilst in the secret chambers of that cocoon. Whilst in that dark night of the soul, we have had to rely entirely on him alone as he gently changed us and taught us about his ways.

Then he gently encourages that butterfly to flap its wings and allow the breeze to carry it up, up and away and he takes delight in all the spectators that marvel at its beauty. I have loved butterflies since I was a child, but when God started to speak to me about the miracle of the metamorphosis, my love for the delicate butterfly grew. Now I look for them every time I venture into the wildlife reserve just behind our house. When I spot one dancing on the breeze, it warms my heart as I know how that little butterfly wears her beauty with pride as she suffered for it. She has undergone a radical transformation and even though her wings are paper thin and delicate, she is also strong and resilient. That butterfly has survived one of God's incredible miracles and that is awe inspiring!

I hope that after reading this book you will take another more in-depth look at butterflies, and I pray too that God will talk to you about this incredible miracle. God talks to us through nature all the time, but are we really listening? Sometimes we become so engrossed in the business of our demanding lives that we forget to look around us and truly hear what our father is saying to us.

For years, God has spoken to me through sunsets. Often when I have had a taxing day and I am feeling downcast, he lights up the sky with a myriad of colour and he reminds me of his love. He has done this countless times and every time I experience this I am swept up in his kindness and grace. I am so thankful to him for reaching out to me in such a beautiful manner.

There could be some out there who may question how I could possibly believe in a good God after the kind of life I've had. Well, my response to that is I know he's good as he has saved me repeatedly. He has embraced me as his own and reminded me that no matter how much I sin, he loves me unconditionally. His grace is sufficient, and I have really learnt that during the course of my life. I continue to learn this every day as I walk with him.

I want to talk a little about my marriage. Honestly, without God's help Kevin and I would have been divorced by now. It is purely through God holding us together and giving us eyes to see each other as he sees us, that has saved our marriage. We were two broken people who came together and tried our best to have a happy marriage, but we had so many odds against us. There were times when we separated but this was always short-lived as we missed each other so much.

Recently, we celebrated our 21st wedding anniversary. That is a miracle within itself. We went away for the weekend and thoroughly enjoyed some quality time together. We realised that in raising two daughters our marriage had taken a back seat and we needed to put it first. It has been challenging to say the least as both our girls are very strong willed and so we've had to be very firm on occasions, but we are getting there. God has done open heart surgery on our marriage, and I can honestly say that I love Kevin more now, than I did on our wedding day.

If you feel stuck in a difficult marriage, I urge you to seek the Lord and not give up. He can come into the situation and transform you so that you can see your spouse through his eyes. This is what God did for me. Even during the most difficult times in my life, when I prayed and asked the Lord to show me Kevin through his eyes, he would do so. He would show me the good, honourable, kind, and loving man that Kevin is and immediately my feelings towards him would change. I have watched as God has worked in my husband and brought healing in areas of his life where he struggled with certain issues. We are now stronger than ever, and I can say without a shadow of a doubt that God has done the work.

One thing I can honestly say from my own experience is that breakthrough only comes when your heart is fully surrendered to God. He loves a contrite heart and if you go to him in reverence and humility and give it all to him, he gets to work. And the beautiful part is that he NEVER disappoints!

As I've penned this book and delved deep into my memory, I have been astounded by God's goodness as I've realised just how instrumental he has been in my life. I want to encourage you that if you have wandered far from him, or if you don't know him, it is never too late. You can change direction today, right now. All you have to do is admit you're a sinner, repent and give your heart to Jesus Christ. He will then come in and do the most amazing metamorphosis in the cocoon you are in. Then he will draw you out and bless you with the most beautiful colours in your wings. As I've said before, the glory belongs to him, and he delights in your individual colours. I am fascinated by butterflies and the fact that every single one is different. Isn't that just so incredible? This loving God that we serve knew that we would take delight in these beautiful creatures, so he got to work creating intricate designs and adding rich, vibrant colours. Our God is the ultimate artist, and he never ceases to amaze me.

Kevin studied Fine Art at University and achieved a distinction. He has painted many beautiful pieces and he is incredibly talented. God has given him this awesome gift and unfortunately, because of the busyness of life he hasn't painted for many years. But I encourage him nevertheless and one day he will start using his gifting again. I am sure of it.

If you don't know God and you have read this far, then my prayer is that you have seen the goodness of the Lord in my life, despite all my mistakes. My desire is for all to come to know my Lord and Saviour.

We are living in turbulent times, and it won't be long before Jesus returns to sweep his bride up into the sky. It is my desire that none be left behind and if I can in some small way encourage non-believers to seek him then my job is done. When I prayed about writing a memoir, God said to me that it must be for his glory. It has taken a great deal of courage as I admit that I fear being judged by those who don't understand or are highly critical. But my pride must be laid down for the greater good. God is not interested in a bruised ego. He cares about how I mirror him. Although I am a work in progress and I have not even nearly arrived, I believe he has used my suffering to transform me into his likeness.

I used to be a very impatient, fractured, and angry person but all these traits have been taken from me. I am now healed, peaceful and a lot more patient (Kevin with testify to this). I still have so much to learn, and I am a work in progress, but I know I will get there with God's help. Every day I am learning to rely more and more on him, and I now trust the Holy Spirit to reveal to me the things that still need to change.

Over the years, God has used me powerfully in the prophetic and this is something that is very close to my heart. It's a gift he's given me that I hold in highest regard as it can either encourage or even damage a person. So, when I pray for someone and God gives me a word or a picture for them, I weigh it very carefully against the Bible so that I am sure it is from him.

Over the years, I have been hurt through false prophesies spoken over my life and for this reason, I take my gift very seriously. I also want to add that it can be a very lonely walk as sometimes it is just me and God. There are times when not even Kevin can understand where I am at. I believe that the Lord sometimes isolates us so that we can lean more heavily on him.

I am so grateful for Kevin as he has helped me so much over the past twenty-three years. He has been my biggest fan but also my greatest critic (in a good way). On many occasions, he has challenged me to grow and when I came out of the cocoon, he has applauded me the most. His belief in me has been so steadfast and I can honestly say that he's been the best thing that ever happened to me.

I am so glad that we stayed the course and stuck it out even during some of the most turbulent times. Our marriage is a testimony to God's grace, and I am certain that without the Lord at the center of our marriage, we would have divorced long ago.

Chapter Twenty-One

There is so much suffering in the world and God is needed now, more than ever. It is my belief and hope that before the rapture happens, there will be a great outpouring of the Holy Spirit and revival will hit the churches. Many will be saved, and I can't wait for that day. I have spent many hours on my knees praying for this as my heart breaks over the situation and the unbelief around me. But I believe in a God who is bigger than all of this and who longs to reconcile everyone to himself. It is his desire that ALL would be saved, and therefore I am confident that he will indeed send his revival fire.

I feel very blessed to be part of a wonderful church where God is really moving. I have met some incredible people, who I now call friends and I am always excited to meet there on a Sunday morning. I think that we will begin to see the Father's heart in the churches as there are so many people out there who have an orphan spirit. I was one of them and so was Kevin. Neither of us felt affirmed or loved as children. Our dads were absent and in fact my mum was as well, so I grew up feeling like an orphan. Kevin has said that he felt the same way.

But our loving heavenly Father changed all of that. Now I feel adopted into his kingdom, and I no longer carry around those orphan feelings. But I look around me, at my friends and colleagues at work and I see so many orphans who need to be adopted by the father. I really believe in the amazing power of prayer. I look back over my life and I can truly see how God has answered my prayers. He knows exactly what we need, and he has always come through for me (even at the last minute).

When certain prayers go unanswered year after year, I have learnt to wait upon God. The Bible clearly states that he is faithful and true and that he hears our prayers, so I keep praying. If you have been waiting for an answer to a specific prayer, then I want to encourage you to keep going. Pray without ceasing and WAIT! God is never late. He is always on time, and he does answer prayer.

I am so passionate about prayer, that I could write a whole book on it. But that's not something I believe God is telling me to do right now. When I first started thinking about writing *Memory in the Mirror*, I put a great deal of prayer into it. I asked God to bless my words and to use them to draw readers to his heart. This is my greatest desire – that others would come to know him through the pages of my book. My other prayer was for all the broken and hurting women out there who are still in their cocoons. My hope is that they would be released from these and that God would reveal himself mightily to them. If the Lord can do it for me, then he can do it for absolutely anyone.

I hope this book has made you think a little more about butterflies and cocoons. The next time you see a butterfly, marvel at its colours and the fact that its colours are made for others to view. That butterfly cannot see it's colour – only you and God can. And the most amazing part of all is that your colours are unique to you. No other butterfly in the world has the exact same design or colours that you have. God has given you talents and abilities that he wants to use. Perhaps you don't know what these are, or you don't think you have anything to offer. But I want to say that you do. Pray and ask the Father to reveal what these are. It may take a while, but I promise you that he will show you.

I want to thank you for joining me on my journey. I hope that you have been encouraged and blessed by this book. My prayer is that you have sought God, or if you are a believer that you have grown closer to him. If you are in a cocoon, then I pray God will release you so that you can shine with his glory and display your awesome colours for all to see. May you know the deep, abiding, and unconditional love of God. I pray that you will step into your destiny in him and leave all your fears behind. Yes, the best is still to come so be brave. Be adventurous! Flap your little butterfly wings and climb higher as you dance gently on the thermals. And most of all know that God sees you and smiles!

Chapter Twenty-Two

There have been occasions in my life where I have confided in friends about my traumatic childhood and turbulent life. One of them told me I'm the bravest person she knows. But what does this mean?

I think it takes courage to look adversity in the face and refuse to be owned by it. I believe that brave is something we become through the school of hard knocks. We can either get better or get bitter and it takes bravery to get better. When I look back over my life, I am grateful for the experiences I've had and the lessons I learned. I don't feel like a victim, I feel victorious! Without them I would not be the person I am. My suffering has deepened me and given me empathy and compassion for others suffering a similar fate. Through the hardships I have become a better listener – more in tune to the cry of other's hearts. I have no time for shallowness and pretense and instead I am drawn to people who have scars. Deep calls unto deep.

I have realised that there are many who simply won't understand and that's OK. If a person has lived a relatively sheltered life with little or no trauma, then how can that person possibly understand? When I meet people like this, I find myself thanking God that they haven't suffered the way I have. This also leads me to another topic that is close to my heart – judgement.

I am under no illusion that there may be people who judge my journey and the mistakes I've made. There may even be family members who criticise this book. It's to be expected, I suppose and that's OK too. There's a saying that goes *never judge someone until you've walked a mile in their shoes.* I love this as it explains judgement so perfectly and this is how I try to live my life. I believe we should be resolute in our desire to never judge a person as we simply do not know what they may be dealing with. I know there will be those who judge my decision to have an abortion all those years ago. That's expected too. But one thing I do know for sure is that having gone through the emotional fallout afterwards, I really paid the price for that one wrong decision. It took me many years to get to a place where I could speak out about the abortion. I buried it and only my immediate family and a couple of close friends knew about it. I lived in an acute state of shame and guilt for many years.

But when God spoke to me about writing my memoir, he reminded me that I would need to be brave, vulnerable, honest, and open. These qualities are required to tell my story authentically. If I can reach out to even one woman who has suffered emotionally following an abortion, then I will be happy that my job is done.

I also want to caution you to not judge those who struggle with mental illness as they already judge themselves very harshly. I know that even though it is more widely accepted and spoken about, there is still an element of taboo surrounding the topic. As

I said before, even to this day only my immediate family and best friends know that I suffer from bipolar disorder.

Growing up with a mum with mental illness and watching how she was branded 'a fruitcake' I vowed to myself that I would never be so cruel and full of judgement. People with mental illness are battling a force that is larger than them. A black dog that pursues them morning, noon, and night. Crippling fatigue and a sense of being in a dark fog. Then there's the social anxiety, panic attacks and aching body to contend with. And one of the other symptoms that so typifies mental illness is chronic self-esteem issues.

I want to crack open the whole subject of suicide as I know this is also judged very harshly. When someone is suicidal, they are not looking for attention. They are not being dramatic or over the top. They are simply in the most agonising pain, and they cannot see a way out. A person contemplating suicide does not want to hurt their loves ones. In fact, they truly believe that their family and friends would be better off without them. They feel like a burden as they're always sad. Often when in a crowd of people, they feel desperately lonely as they struggle to connect with others.

Robin Williams was one of my favourite actors and I've seen all his films. When he committed suicide a few years ago I was gutted – devastated. Such a beautiful soul with incredible wit and talent gone too soon. He also struggled with bipolar disorder and like I said I guess the pain and the loneliness simply became too much.

If you know someone who is suicidal, please don't be trite. Don't say things such as 'pull yourself together,' or 'chin up.' These comments just make a depressed person feel even worse. If it were that simple, then they'd do it. But the reality is that they simply cannot just snap out of it. They need help and they also need your compassion and empathy.

When I've been at my lowest, just getting out of the bed in the morning has been a huge challenge. That's when the darkness would consume me the most. But it was at those times that I called on the power of prayer. When I could feel the mist rolling in, I would speak scripture out loud. *God has not given me a spirit of fear, but of strength, courage, and a sound mind.*

I found this reassuring and it immediately strengthened me. As I mentioned previously, I am so much better now and the medication I am on is working. But that doesn't mean that I don't occasionally have the odd bad day where everything, even the most menial tasks like washing my hair feels overwhelming. On days like that, I feel like my skin is being pricked by a million tiny needles and all my senses are on high alert. I'm grateful that I have a job that I love as it forces me to get out of bed every morning and just crack on.

But when those dark days do come, I have learnt how to manage them. If I can, I reschedule meetings and I ease myself gently into my work. I don't bite off more than I can chew. I've learnt to affirm myself and believe that life is wonderful and good things are still to come. I am not put off by all the awful events that I have experienced. That's all in the past now and it's dead and buried. Instead, I focus on the future and the fact that my worst days are behind me. I am a warrior princess of the King, and he has an amazing destiny for me.

I am so grateful that I have been set free from fear. As I've mentioned before, this is something that followed me most of my life like a stray dog. It was constant. Always there. Slowly it would suffocate me and force the air out of my lungs until I was nothing but a blithering wreck. I used to suffer from crippling panic attacks where my heart would race, and I would hyperventilate.

Life in general scared me. But most people had no idea that I suffered this way. I learnt to hide it behind a bubbly, outgoing personality. Instead of focusing on my fear, I would crack jokes with friends over a glass of wine. I learnt to put on a persona that would convince others that I was fine. But behind the mask, I was anything but.

About a year ago, God started to speak to me about the fear. He told me that it was not his will for me to live under its tyranny. I said I knew that but didn't know how to get rid of it. That's when he showed me that I need to attack it with the Word of God and really, truly believe what scripture says about me. As I started to do this, I realised that I could be free and that was God's intention for me. He also spoke to me about being a warrior princess and told me that the battle is fierce as there is an enemy of our souls. Satan didn't want me to be set free from fear as he was afraid that I would in turn help others who were afflicted with fear too. As I learnt to apply scripture to my life and declare it out loud, a shift slowly started to happen. But that's not to say that I don't occasionally have days where the fear tries to return. But when it does, I know exactly what to do. I use my sword to cut the enemies ploys and I declare life giving words over my life.

It also says in the Bible that we have the power of life or death in the tongue. Kevin has often spoken to me about this. He always says that we must watch our words and be very careful about what we say. We can either bless or curse with our words and it's so important to remember that.

I also believe in kindness. If I was asked what the most important trait in a person is, I would say it's kindness. There is too much nastiness in this world and not nearly enough kindness. I think this trait also develops out of deep suffering. Some of the kindest people I know have gone through deep pain and it has resulted in the beautiful fragrance of genuine, unadulterated kindness.

I think that is one of the characteristics of God that I love the most. He is an incredibly kind and loving Father. In the first instance, he is the one who has taught me the most about kindness and even though I don't always get it right, I try to be as kind to others as I possibly can. And the beauty of it is that it doesn't have to cost us anything. Just giving a friend a reassuring hug or listening ear are beautiful ways to extend kindness into the world.

As I come to the end of *Memory in the Mirror,* I'd like to thank you for joining me on my journey. I hope that God has spoken to you and that you are encouraged. My prayer for you is that you would know how high and how wide the father's love is for you. Additionally, I pray that whatever hard place you are going through right now would be replaced with a wide, open, and peaceful space where you can breathe again.

May you fly high above the cares of this world and be brave enough to allow others to view the beautiful colours of your wings. God delights in you and the best is yet to come!

Printed in Great Britain
by Amazon